Music fro[...]

NED ROREM

Readers of Ned R[...] *[...] Diary* will find *Music from Inside Out* a quite different kind of book. The former was, in effect, a portrait of the composer as a young man in Paris of the fifties. The present book is the author's attempt to answer people's questions about composers and music, to show "from inside out" the how and the why of music.

"A composer, when he is not composing," writes Mr. Rorem, "has only a finite number of artistic considerations on his mind, and sooner or later he puts these considerations into words. They deal less with the so-called concerns of creation than with how to answer other people's questions about those concerns. Over the years he learns to give replies (if not answers) to the questions, while remaining aware, like Mendelssohn, that 'it's not that music is too imprecise for words, but too precise.' "

Several years ago, Mr. Rorem was invited to give a number of lectures at Buffalo University, for a lay audience, followed by concerts of his own devising. "What did I know about music except how to write it?" he says. "For the first time I was required to consider my craft without using my ear. The ear is subtler than the eye. Seeing is believing, hearing is understanding. But understanding what? Does one *understand* music?

has been [...]
American universities, the most recent of which is the University of Utah, and his music has been performed by many of our leading orchestras.

Music from Inside Out

By the same author

The Paris Diary of Ned Rorem

BY NED ROREM

Music
from Inside Out

GEORGE BRAZILLER
NEW YORK

To my mother and father
Gladys and Rufus Rorem
and to my sister
Rosemary Marshall

Author's Note

Seven of these chapters were first presented as lectures under
the bequest of the Slee Foundation at Buffalo University in
1959 and 1960. They were subsequently published by the following periodicals:

The American Record Guide: "Writing Songs," "Song and
Singer," "Composer and Performance," "Is New Music New?,"
and "Pictures and Pieces." (The last two were reprinted in *The
London Magazine* and, in Italian, in *Discoteca.*)

Music Journal: "Listening and Hearing" and "Four Questions
Answered."

The article on Poulenc was written for *The Village Voice*, and
reprinted in London's *Tempo*, on the occasion of the composer's
death in 1963. The review of Honegger's book appeared in the
Sunday *New York Times*, August 1966.

"Random Notes" appeared in *Commentary*, November 1966.

"Anatomy of Two Songs" (from my 1949 diary) is printed
here for the first time.

In the Appendix, I have listed chronologically the musical
programs which succeeded each Buffalo lecture, and have included the names of all the performing musicians who so
wonderfully helped me there.

The fragments of dedicatory verse used as epigrams are all
from poems I have set to music.

N.R.

Contents

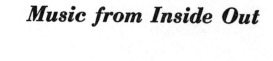

Music from Inside Out

Theme

A composer when he is not composing has only a finite number of artistic considerations on his mind, and sooner or later he puts these considerations into words. They deal less with the so-called concerns of creation than with how to answer other people's questions about those concerns. Over the years he learns to give replies (if not answers) to the questions, while remaining aware, like Mendelssohn, that "it's not that music is too imprecise for words, but too precise."

My own replies had always been voiced in undisciplined privacy. Suddenly in 1959 I was forced to formalize them onto paper, then re-express them aloud to a captive audience. Having until then lived by the precept *Teachers know—Composers do*, I was uneasy at Buffalo University's invitation to deliver seven lectures. What did I know about music except how to write it? For the first time I was required to consider my craft without using my ear.

The ear is a subtler mechanism than the eye. Seeing is believing, hearing is understanding. But understanding what? Does one *understand* music? As for speech, it is usually—as uttered by musicians as by everyone else—pure babble. Nevertheless I agreed to speak, hoping that in the allotted time my babble might grow coherent.

1

The speeches were to be for a lay public, and followed by concerts of my own devising. The devising part was immediately clear: I would feature only music of the twentieth century, since this music was my chief reason for living, and since the century belonged also to my audience. Yet these people were typically geared—from the outside in, so to speak—toward the art of their time, appraising it with apprehension if not downright terror. I wished to help turn their terror into pleasure.

How that help might be verbally organized was less immediately clear. I did not wish to offer program notes on the music, yet I did hope to show—from the inside out—why such music came to be.

My organizing theme was built on the assumption that what layman and student alike find most mysterious about a composer is his ear (can he really *hear* all those notes in his head?). My variations on this theme were developed in the knowledge that at least one composer's hearing was not too mysterious, and that it might be elucidated through his visual attitudes, his opinions of the then current scene, a businesslike approach toward a compositional form, suggestions as to how others could develop satisfying listening habits, recounting of how a piece comes to be played after it's composed, and candid answers to even more commonplace queries.

What I learned while formulating these essays is uncertain: my music did not change nor did my thoughts grow more conclusive. Those inconclusive thoughts, however, become orderly, and order is always helpful for teaching, which most composers are called on to do now and then.

After an interval of some seven years, while reassessing this material for publication in book form, I find with a rather bemused detachment that I still agree with the general basic tone. On the other hand, many specifics (particularly illustrations of ideas by "timely" examples) seem already outmoded, and also the superficial intellectual tone of today is altered (I am writing in 1966). For instance, I spoke in these lectures a good deal about Art and Artists as isolated interests. The current attitude—perhaps even my own—no longer capitalizes these phenomena: art is where you find it, in Bach or the Beatles, not falsely sanctified. Since the Industrial Revolution until our mid-century point, the cultured public had grown increasingly disseminated and elite; today the public itself is artist-participant, not judge. There's no longer good and bad art, just good and bad.

I toyed with the possibility of updating various passages, but decided against it. The decision was made partly because I'd no further heart to paraphrase old matters and would prefer to think on new ones, but also because the very updating could so soon in turn grow *démodé*. Elsewhere in this book I've noted that "our civilization seems unique because of its smaller subdivisions. Concepts disappear and are replaced so rapidly that generations shorten to decades." (Today I'm even inclined to change decades to maybe four years.) So I've left everything intact: each cliché or hopefully wise view must fend for itself just as a musical work must finally prove its own terms without its composer's apologies.

As a light finale to the possibly ponderous theme of the Buffalo lectures, I have appended two personal recollections, and a coda of notes from my recent diary. An occasional footnote will situate the quaintness of some 1959 terminology, or clarify the fact that these talks were originally written—unlike some modern music—to be heard and not seen.

N.R.

Music for the Eye
and the Mind

sound n . . . b) a particular auditory impression.
—*Webster's*

"The essential feature of sound . . . is not its location, but that it *be*, that it fill space . . . The concertgoer closes his eyes."
—*Marshall McLuhan*

"Music should be heard with the eyes open."
—*Igor Stravinsky*

"I would like to sound a word of warning to Mr. McLuhan: to speak is to lie. To lie is to collaborate."
—*John Cage*

"[Cage's] work represents . . . not only the most advanced methods now in use anywhere but original musical expression of the very highest poetic quality."
—*Virgil Thomson* (1945)

"[Thomson's] music has today little place. For all his heterodoxical use of the twelve tones, merely providing dodecaphony with a harmonic outlet does not seem to me to be the necessary facing of contemporary musical reality."
—*John Cage* (1958)

"Success will not wholly pass by the rhythmic experimenters. . . I can imagine them making lovely scores for all the better films about space travel. . . And we shall all be very happy."
—*Virgil Thomson* (1959)

"The sound of music—as opposed to rustling leaves or words of love—is sensual only secondarily. First it must make sense."
—*Ned Rorem*

1

Pictures and Pieces

It is idle though not really odious to compare the arts, and people are always doing it. But they usually generalize on like- ness, not disparity, lumping together all arts whose practi- tioners supposedly represent that portion of society which best enjoys "the gift of self-realization." No two expressions are more opposed than music and painting. Their function, the manner of their making, the characters of the workmen them- selves are as dissimilar as the needs of their respective publics.

In childhood I believed that a given artist could have de- veloped into any other kind—that he had only to choose between, say, prose or sculpture. Certainly all children are all things, close to natural truth and the origins of philosophy. Maturity's manners later stunt the imagination which had held a fantastic door ajar; to the more calloused this door closes forever. Composers and painters, in retaining initial fancies, stay children. That seems their sole point in common, as though mutual receptivity had been smothered in adolescence. A fair percentage of plastic artists appear all but tone-deaf and some fine musicians are not a bit visual.

Picasso, for example, typical of most people, is not very reactive to sound about him; his ears prefer the Iberian nos- talgia of bullfight trumpets to more sophisticated music. But

his eyes are black diamond bullets which never miss their mark
yet never find repose.

Many a musician is oblivious to scenes before him. He too
resembles most laymen in that years pass blindly, though he
knows the pitch of an auto horn, a robin's cry, a faucet dripping
blocks away.

Those examples concern just eyes and ears because the Fine
Arts are all devoted to only sight and hearing. Some permit
alternate use of these two senses, but exclusivity is reserved
for painting and music, which present polar extremes of the
seven arts.[1]

In a progressive Manhattan kindergarten (the kind that
encourages imagination at any price), I once heard an art
instructress comment: "But Johnny, your tree *looks* like a tree!
I'll have to fail you. . . ." On the other hand I hear frequent
cries that music has forsaken melody and grown abstract. It
was always abstract. The complaint is really lodged against a
lack of familiar tunes in new pieces. Familiar tunes, being
music, are also abstract even when using words. Words help
recall tunes, thus making them familiar, but it is the verbal
associations only which lend literal sense to sound.

Essentially music is abstract and painting is representational
despite what we hear to the contrary. Music has no intellectual
significance, no meaning outside itself. This is not less true of
so-called programmatic than of absolute music wherein subjective connotations are not intended.

---

[1] No serious art is dedicated to a stimulation of odor, taste, or touch
(though the blind are said to appreciate sculpture). Scriabin, before his
death, projected a *Poem of Mystery* for performance on a mountaintop.
The audience, while listening, was to behold a color screen, eat exotic
foods, inhale perfume, and caress velvet. This forecasted the loving couple
munching popcorn at the movies and would also have proved no more
than pleasurable confusion. It is impossible to react simultaneously to all
five senses in full indulgence. Even the motion-picture addict, as we shall
see, is usually unaware of the musical sound track except—as in musical
comedies—where sound is an end in itself.

I believe that painting does have meaning outside itself. When abstract painters profess a striving to eliminate representation, their very effort implies camouflage.[2] A musician feels no compunction to disguise "subject matter" and might even attempt to reveal it, safely assured that logicians will never decipher and expose his secret thoughts. No inquisition can intelligibly reproach a composer as it can a Goya for subversive or obscene notions.

Richard Strauss once declared himself capable of denoting a fork on a table through sound alone. Certainly his tone poems evoke realistic windmills, bleating sheep, human chatter and such. Any competent orchestrater can simulate worldly noises without much trouble, as a talented mimic can bark like a dog. (Charlie Chaplin, they say, once performed an aria, and beautifully, to everyone's amazement. "I can't really sing at all," he explained later. "I was just doing my Caruso number!") The closer these copies approach reality the farther they retreat from creation. Wilde's paradox: Nature imitates Art.

If we were not informed of Strauss's fork or sheep we'd either invent our own associations or listen as if to "pure" music. If told that these sounds meant knives or sea gulls we'd leave it at that. In music an image is no more than approximate.

Each century gives conventional symbols for general mood. In recent Western music minor means sad, though it had no such suggestion three hundred years ago; even today, who is saddened by the completely minor carol *God Rest You Merry Gentlemen*? The mode of C-major is supposed to be happy, but the Spartans considered it lascivious (which is not always the same thing). We don't disagree on what is termed joyous, tragic, or ecstatic, except when we read into the style of one musical period that which refers to another. In pictures, how-

---

[2] Action Painting is already a school of the past. More recently Robert Indiana's Pop exhibit was promoted by reviving the presumably straightforward music of Virgil Thomson, thirty years Indiana's senior. If Thomson felt surprise at the relationship, he liked the concert. Now Pop Art too is fading though Thomson remains. Such juxtapositions come and go.

ever, a wedding or funeral always mean just that, no matter
when or where they were made.

Music is probably the least international of languages. During
two years in Morocco I never encountered a native who could
fathom our formal music any more than our Christian values.
Only in the past century and to us of the West do Strauss's
sheep or Ravel's sad birds, Respighi's trees or Honegger's engine,
signify themselves in sound through habit and suggestion. And
yet, when he knows what it represents, who, hearing Britten's
Sick Rose, for instance, can restrain a spinal chill when that
wormlike horn bores into the flower's heart? An Arab would not
see this as we do—through the ears. We also, were we not told
beforehand of the intended association, would miss our guess
nine times out of ten even with such broad themes as love and
war, festivity and madness. Scientific experiments have proved
it. Gone are the days when Carl Maria von Weber's diminished-
seventh tremolos will scare anyone.

Music's inherent abstraction is what renders it so malleable
in collaborative fields. A choreographer may mold a narrative
around absolute music, or effectively revise the story line of a
programmatic work. Robbins' ballet on *The Afternoon of a
Faun* is as plausible as Nijinsky's. And Nijinsky's version of
The Rite of Spring was no more catastrophic than Disney's.
Stravinsky's masterpiece, which suffocated both ballet and film,
survives uniquely in concert halls. Music can make or break a
ballet because sound is necessary to the dance. And although
audiences will take a good deal more of the "unfamiliar" in
spectacles which mix the arts than in music alone, when sound
dominates the visual they revolt—as in the famous case of
The Rite of Spring.

Music is less integral to the film medium, so even greater
risks can be run. A musically untutored movie audience accepts
without flinching a score whose audacity, if heard in concert,
would send the elite yelling for mercy. The public is, and should

be, mostly unconscious of movie music; a background fails when it distracts from central business. But such is music's strength that it may sugarcoat a tasteless film or poison one of quality. A recent drama of capital punishment, *I Want to Live*, excited extra tension through its sound-track of progressive jazz. *On the Beach*, whose subject was more timely still (terrestrial death through radioactivity), was devitalized by a score with old-fashioned associations.

Any music may persuasively accompany any image or story while inevitably dictating the *tone* of the joint effort. Music's power lies in an absence of human significance and this power dominates all mediums it contacts. When Auric composed the score for Jean Cocteau's film, *The Blood of a Poet*, he produced what is commonly known as love music for love scenes, game music for game scenes, funeral music for funeral scenes. Cocteau had the bright idea of replacing the love music with the funeral, game music with the love, funeral with game. And it worked—like prosciutto and melon. Nor did Cocteau commission a composer for his ballet of a modern young painter who hangs himself on stage; he used a passacaglia of Bach whose clash with the present ignited the eternal.

The sea reminds me of Debussy's *La Mer*—*La Mer* never reminds me of the sea. But if a picture recalls the sea, the sea conjures up no picture of anything beyond itself. In this sense water is as abstract as music, but a picture of water *represents* an abstraction. Whatever title Debussy may have chosen, his work is finally enjoyed as sheer music (though the earmarks of *La Mer* have so often been imitated for cinematic seascapes that the original now contains non-musical connotations). If a novice were told that the three movements of this piece illustrated three times of day, not on the sea but in a city, he wouldn't know the difference. Paintings also present different impressions to different people: as many interpretations exist as spectators. But I am speaking now of creative consciousness, not audience effect. At bottom a composer cannot work through visions. Painters, whether or not they're aware of it, always paint a picture of *something*. Some attempt to divorce nature and search for a plane as abstract as music's. While avoiding a title more committal than *Conception in Green* or *Study No. 2,* they are actually depicting tangibles which, like clouds, assume logical shape. Since a composer's auditor never has subject matter to cling to, hints may be dropped about some subjective idea as symbolic guide through an unknown formal region. To both artists the title is a forethought or afterthought extraneous to actual work. Human ideas are dissolved by music on its highest level, just as they are evolved by pictures. That is the reason it's easier to envisage an artist himself through his pictures than through his pieces.

The evocative title for other than vocal music has been alternately in and out of vogue since the fifteenth century. Debussy happened to be born to a period when descriptive music was stylish. Not only in *La Mer* but in his entire output he is linked with Impressionism, the only movement in which pictorial and sonic arts have tried meeting on common ground. Impressionism really has little to do with music. It names the desire of a group of nineteenth-century French painters to elicit an *impression* and avoid a clear-cut message. Since music never conveys (as painting can) a clear-cut message, it is always in a way impressionistic and hence need not be singled out as such. The painting's concern with illumination of a subject rather than the subject itself emphasized light rather than what was lighted. Now music has no color: at best the term "timbre" applies for varieties of sound combination. Musically "light" or "dark" tones are mere figures of speech.

The current Zen trend toward the Nowness of things relates to pictorial impressionism. Painters captured a momentary effect, a vague definition, a tree glimpsed through shifting fog at too close or far a distance for usual meaning. Monet's *Water Lilies* form a mental picture retreating as much as possible from physical resemblance while still retaining identity. Debussy stressed the same mood inversely by attempting to make sounds signify sights. Though their impressionistic aims appear synonymous, the devices of these men are not comparable because of a non-common language. Whether they succeeded in sharing their reactions with the public is unimportant so long as the result was complete in itself.

Rendition of things out of focus or as they exist for the fraction of a second is nevertheless rendition of *things*. Such things from new distances assume new meanings. A man is only visibly a man while in speaking range. A mile off he is a dot representing a man, an inch away he grows more than human. On this level the term "abstract" is not absurd for pictures because they can represent an abstraction of the specific. (If music represents an abstraction of the specific it has never been demonstrated.) The phrase "non-representational" is nonetheless inappropriate and should perhaps be substituted by "non-literal."

Single fields of vision force the eye to focus on but one object at a time; surroundings of that object are blurred. Impressionist painters concentrated on the blur seeking atmosphere rather than fine clarification.[3] Debussy sought to clarify the blur. He pulverized sound into a prismatic mist like the confettied *pointillist* close-ups that produce a haze of overall coherence. Indeed, he achieved formal freedom in a manner hard to analyze, and longed to eliminate beginnings and ends from his art and retain only middles. Music naturally exists in time, so must start and stop in time. Painting also starts and stops, but in space and with no climax in the accumu-

[3] In music a "surface" theme is seized by the ear, which takes accompaniment as much for granted as the eye takes *La Gioconda*'s background. But the comparison is not what musical impressionists had in mind.

lative mobile sense. Climaxes are indigenous to all the "time arts," including dance which, though manifest in space like sculpture, is basically a moving picture.

Painting's symbolic "climax" is the static focal point which is always immediate—music's real climax is always kept waiting. Painters emulate time by copying recollections of a split moment as the Impressionists did, or like the realist portrait painter whose subject sits immobile for days to be reconstructed from the composite of a million moments. The portraitist's eye disintegrates his model into fragments which his hand reassembles on canvas. The subject *feels* his dismembered sections float across the studio, controlled by the painter's magnet vision; like flies in amber they come to rest in oil. If the artist steals of his model forever, the model takes also from the artist: such relationships are never one-sided. But the union's pictorial result is frozen.

Music exists—not on canvas nor yet on the staff—only in motion. The good listener will hear it as the present prolonged. The good spectator will see a picture also as a whole even when he examines at close range images recreated from a distance, or from a distance images made at close range. Since a finished picture does not rely on time, the individual has more *time* to inspect it, whereas music's meaning (if any) must be caught on the run.

An entire painting is absorbed at the speed of light. The time it takes our eye to reach the canvas is all that's required for an image to be stamped indelibly on the brain. We seem to look into it, yet its third dimension is imaginary; we cannot penetrate increasingly as into the universe. We come to know it in many ways, each of which constitutes an indivisible moment of the present. . . . A whole piece of music is grasped only in retrospect. Were it feasible to condense a piece for performance at an infinite speed (say, a whole symphony lasting one second), time would still be the leading factor and the audience would still have to remain till the end without having *seen* the music as a static image. We can look away from pictures but we can't listen away from sounds. We accept in simile "the image of sound" yet we never speak of "the sound of image."[4]

To convey through music a non-musical idea three formulas are available: the tone picture, the tone poem, and the incidental background for plays.

Tone pictures are puns which never need explanation to be enjoyed. The majority refer to aspects of nature, usually water or birds, or vistas including both, in specified attitudes at specified times of day. They may use the same title without necessarily sounding alike. How many pieces are called The Fountain! More rare are resemblant musics with diverse significance. The opening measures of Debussy's *Clouds*, of Moussorgsky's *Four Walls*, and of Stravinsky's *Nightingale* are too similar for coincidence, yet their literary intentions are unrelated. Different means are tried for the same subject and the same means for different subjects, but the musician won't name a work "Abstraction"—he doesn't have to. Nevertheless, he can't truly expect us to see sounds any more than we hear paint. A sonorous landscape by any other name would sound as sweet.

Tone poems tell stories. They involve direct emotions indirectly transported on wings of wordless song through fire, jealousy, and death. Like good tone pictures, they possess abstract coherence without a program.

The third division, the incidental background for plays, in turn serves three purposes, all very general. The first is for indicating weather conditions and originates from the tone picture; the second is for love scenes and derives from the tone poem; the last is for quieting the audience or getting actors on

---

[4] Exceptions to these principles of perception are artificially provoked. With marihuana the aurally uninitiated will *witness* simultaneously independent counterpoints. With mescalin the optically unresponsive will *enter* a canvas, like Alice in the mirror, and recreate with the artist each layer of his working process.

and off stage, and stems from the military fanfare. Music is never more explicit.

Actual paintings sometimes inspire music. The most famous example is *Pictures at an Exhibition*. And just this season [1960] new works by Diamond and Schuller used paintings of Paul Klee as "theme." Klee himself once said: "Art does not render the visible, but renders visible." He was speaking, I imagine, only of plastic art. It remains doubtful that his painting is rendered more visible as interpreted through an unrelated medium. Hindemith maintains that "the reactions music evokes are not feelings, but . . . memories of feelings." If a composer enjoins us to recall emotions about a picture, he distracts attention from his piece, since concentration is not wholly directed to more than one thing at a time.

Dallapiccola arranges notes on a staff to look like the Cross of Christ. Of course we don't hear a cross any more than we see tomorrow. If impatience leads us to conclude that certain music, like children, should be seen and not heard, Dallapiccola's device is not for that disqualified. Do the typographical designs of Cummings' poetry disturb it when read aloud? or does the holy 3 of liturgical chant oblige us to feel the Trinity rather than a metrical pulse? Tricks are valid when used as cause and not effect. We judge by expressive results. . . . Virgil Thomson has posed people for musical portraits. This too is a means to an end like re-evaluating pictures by sound. The tonal image provides impetus to build an ultimate abstraction.

In like manner a painter on a dull day may get himself going by drawing geometric forms which eventually become representational. To Mondrian or Albers the geometric presents an end in itself. Dare I say this end is also representational? (Skeptics maintain such painting is merely unfinished while Freudians find in it God knows how many symbols.) Of course it is representational: nature abounds in geometry as she abounds in vibrations from which music is fashioned; yet psychoanalysts are shy of chords and scales. (It would be amusing to speculate about Ravel's fixation on the descending fourth whenever he sets the word *maman* to music!)

I too have written visual music, for I don't always practice what I preach. In a work called *Eagles for Orchestra* I followed a word picture of Whitman, but soon dispensed with all thought of birds and was impelled only by the flow of verse. Poetry, falling between the poles of sight and sound, supplies both image and movement. Still, I never see eagles when I hear my music, which could as easily represent a hurricane, or heavy traffic, or nothing at all. I used the title just because it's pretty.

Aesthetic difference in intention no doubt contributes to personality difference between makers of pictures and pieces. There are also practical reasons.

Painters don't need verbal articulation. Addressing the sense of sight through the sense of touch, they make by contact with canvas what will be seen. Doubly involved with the sensual, they are unconcerned with intellectual justification. Besides, they often have poets as spokesmen. Trends like Surrealism, which are considered the painters' private property, are primarily literary movements which take up painters. None of these movements has ever dealt positively with music.

Composers as a race are more lucid. What we call a "primitive" in painting (one without formal experience) is unimaginable in musical composition, which is a craft whose elements are not implicit in the growing-up process. Everyone from birth learns to speak and use his hands, and literally anyone can write poems or draw pictures (drawing is a kind of writing, and vice versa). But certain rudiments of composition must be encased before a minimal expression is plausible, because music requires an interpreter to whom the creator's intention must be clear. Painting presupposes no interpretation other than by the spectator; it needs no performing middleman.

On its lowest plane the pictorial is more accessible than the sonorous—the eye is a less complex instrument than the ear— so there are more painters around than composers. In Paris alone forty thousand are inscribed in the city census; not even a fifth that number of composers exists in the world. Quality, of course, smooths out the difference; each field claims the same small number of superior artists. . . . Financially again the balance is unequal. A professional painter earns directly through his work many times more than a composer of corresponding age and reputation. As a palpable commodity, painting is a practical investment; music cannot be owned and hence lacks market value. The composer needs not only communication with his interpreter, but must develop extra-compositional articulation to earn a living. The painter spends much of his time dealing directly with his public, which the composer seldom does.

The formal aspects of painting and music contain noncomparable dimensions, but their embellishments—color and orchestration—are not dissimilar. Red cannot exist by itself (it cannot be conscious of itself, so to speak) without being a red something; nor can a flute sound be just that: it will always be a flute playing something. This is a relation, if not an infallible one, for color can indicate form in painting while orchestration plays no formal part in music.

The element of professional *rapprochement* between these arts is happiest in the theater where the wedding is of mediums rather than of artists. Frequently the musician and set designer never meet. Their products are soldered together by a director upon whose talent the success of the marriage depends. It is rare that painter and composer collaborate freely as do poet and painter or composer and poet.

A given artist is usually well versed in one of the sister arts which he enjoys as a hobby. Musicians and painters, nonetheless, don't seem to need each other. Their chief similarity as private citizens is in mutual disregard. Creative Jacks-of-all-trades, from Leonardo to Noel Coward, have always been something of a rarity, and are becoming more so. This is not reprehensible: to a creator vast knowledge is unnecessary, sometimes even harmful.

Artists, like children, resist alienation from nature. None seek to copy so much as to join nature by opening a glass door to which they alone hold the key, but through which others can look. Painting's connection with nature (whether geometric or photographic) is more apparent than music's. The latter, like architecture, proceeds in indirect simulation by subduing inspiration to calculation. Its "unnatural" components are what render it the abstractest art, for one musical sound has meaning only in ordered relation to another, while in nature sound has unordered meaning in itself.

The truest relation between artists is not as thinkers but as doers obsessed with organized self-discovery. Composer and painter alike feel toward the tools of their expression as interpreters toward their instrument. The disheveled neatness atop the piano, the easel and chisel, pencil and paper, the assemblage of colors and staves and inks and rulers are as tenderly disinterested and aggravating as twins to these men. Both of them while working inhabit a strenuous cocoon removed from time and space, the better to deal objectively with space and time—for both share the immediate while in the act of making. The logic of hindsight alone demonstrates their dissimilar intentions.

To dispel a fallacy I have shown art as a fluid matter not to be judged by stagnant standards. My premise has been that music and painting are less resemblant than generally supposed. Any theory which questions bromides is always partly valid. Sometime I'll try proving that music is never abstract, painting always is. Such an approach merged with the present one might allow that pictures and pieces are really the same. A discouraging assumption. After all, if the arts could express each other we wouldn't need more than one.

Buffalo, 1959

2
Is New Music New?

Like our ancestors we will finally be judged by our culture, and by the arts which are that culture's issue. But today's civilization seems unique because of its smaller subdivisions. Concepts disappear and are replaced so rapidly that generations shorten to decades. In art as in engineering, Monday's triumph becomes Tuesday's cliché. The shrinking time-span leads to mass specialization, which in turn makes culture stress more than ever the power of novelty.

What is novelty? Can it be represented by substitution, by improvement? In art, at least, there is no improvement, no substitution, although the properties of creation are never identical. We cannot have meaning except in relation to the past. Now the past grows harder to pinpoint with the present so subject to change. The 1900's, however, have reached a peak high enough to survey the last sixty years and to speculate on the next forty. From that height one observes a recent recapitulation of the first half-century.

The recapitulation began with the atomic explosion of 1945. Children of that time were weaned into an era accepting incredible facts of science as casually as children of the first war accepted facts of fiction. Today's youth replaces art with scientific imagination; even science-fiction lacks luster next to

23

realities of space travel. Space is the new romance while art appears unreal, though, of course, it is no more unreal than mysteries found through a telescope, than attitudes maintained through tranquilizers. Reality fluctuates as science progresses, and though the latter's function is to instruct, art's is to reflect; and any art, no matter how apparently off-center, necessarily mirrors its period of production.

Still, for a lot of people our music sounds very confused indeed, as though to balance with a shifty present it needed to force itself toward new approaches. How new these actually are we shall try to discover.

There are three dominant trends in modern composition: jazz, experimental, and conservative.

The present state of jazz recalls Madame Chanel's remark: "Fashion is beauty growing ugly, art is ugliness growing beautiful." If her *bon mot* holds true it seems especially to do so in the art of jazz, whose very nature interrelates composer, performer, and audience more than other music does. Here composition changes with each performance, performance styles alter as frequently as Chanel's, and these styles are usually initiated by the chief consumer: youth. At present, youth accents deep listening without song or dance.[1] The frenzy jazz once provoked has subsided. But what appears "cool" probably applies to the frail crust protecting warm hearts. Warm or cool, these young hearts are in dead earnest about what they hear as a workable innovation, namely, the fusion of jazz and classical procedures.

Today is always tomorrow's yesterday. How quickly the life and death of Ma Rainey, of Bessie Smith, even of Billie Holiday, became souvenirs to the middle-aged, while to most young they

---

[1] Now, only six years later, dance is very much back, but dance which frantically celebrates the self and not the partner.

are not even legends.[2] Yet their vocal styles swept a continent and were deeply felt by many a symphonist.

In America, jazz and so-called serious music were planted and grew simultaneously from quite independent seeds. Yet from the start men like Gottschalk borrowed elements of the same slave songs that evolved into Blues. At the turn of the century MacDowell, a comparative sophisticate, was taking heavily from Negro tunes; and by 1914 others such as Carpenter were writing what they frankly called symphonic jazz. The plant had bloomed, spreading wildly through the states and overseas. During the twenties it was particularly fruitful for concert composers including Ravel and Milhaud, Gershwin and Copland.

But the jazzness of jazz eluded them all. The French just translated the trimmings into their language, which remained essentially French. Gershwin lacked technique for integration, his larger pieces being at best medleys of marvelous pop songs. As for Copland, his was an intellectual attempt to shake off European influences by Americanizing his palette with local colors. He was better equipped than Gershwin for patterning solid pieces from folk ideas, but they too sounded more Gallic than Negro, more like the Frenchified version than the real thing. For though each of these men grew up where sounds of jazz were daily fare, none sprang from the environment which had created such sounds of necessity.

Ten years later the jazz world itself fell into a reverse trap by obliging larger shapes onto its improvisatory style. Improvisation is best when brief. An ambitious fantasy of, say, Duke Ellington sounds less like a tight construction than a disjointed rhapsody, and retains the virtues of neither.

The demarcation point between the two musics blurs increasingly now when the jazz man is more often an Ivy Leaguer than a poor Negro born to the tradition of jam sessions.[3] Like

[2] Billie, of course, has since come in for a big revival.
[3] The Beatles were in diapers when this was written.

his predecessors, he seeks to reconcile a natural penchant for jazz with a cultivated training in composition.

Jazz is a player's art, not a composer's. Or better, composer and player are one: their simultaneous execution is changeable, the performer is master. What we call classical is an unchangeable expression whose performer must be servant. To some these distinctions represent artistic aims that remain psychologically divorced. Others find them hairsplitting, since music is music after all, and its multiple aspects are uniting.

If jazz and classical are the same it should be self-evident. Then why breed them like horse and donkey? The mule is complete in itself (thought it cannot reproduce), while jazz combined with classical always sounds like jazz combined with classical, not like a unified offspring. One cannot mate inherent rigidity with inherent looseness. These musics have always traded casual mannerisms, but in their grander unions either the spontaneity is stifled by restriction or the framework crumbles from the spontaneity.

Jazz performers are always being termed "ahead of their time." Could it be the public who's behind the times? Actually both are of their time since reaction and progress must exist together as polar forces impelling any generation. But the *compositional* progress claimed by the "progressive" Brubeck's and Kenton's is speculative: their harmony is usually of the Debussyists, their melody basically Schubertian, their rhythm behind Stravinsky's of fifty years back, and their counterpoint clearly modeled on Bach's. Only in scoring are they "ahead of the times," an overhauling of orchestral method being jazz's prime contribution.

But that contribution is no small matter. The sound is inimitably one of jazz itself, and sound after all is the heart of music. Not only instrumental innovation but the never-duplicated manner of its execution is what makes jazz jazz. Special instruments are played in special fashion: it is not the tune but the *way* with a tune, not the basic material but the coloration which identifies this music. And collective improvisation has no counterpart in classical realms. Jazz musicians are not "interpreters" but creative executants—a taboo cognomen for "long hair" performers who presumably obey the composer's dictates.

The status of jazz has risen quickly and no musician of any breed is entirely immune to it. Maybe it is the vital music of today. But the vitality has been there from the start.

The experimentalists are of three schools: serial, electronic, and chance. Their aims are not unrelated and their practitioners on fairly good terms.[4]

Serial composers are the progeny of Schoenberg, who originally codified chromaticism into the twelve-tone series technique. His followers have systematized not only tones but every variable of sound. The result, known as integral serialism, is hailed by Křenek as "the composer's liberation from the dictatorship of inspiration."

If the health of jazz lies in its attraction to the ear, some maintain that serial music appeals only to the eye. Indeed, antagonists say that the rightness of serial sound relations is less important than the rightness of theoretic relations, since it is all mathematically predetermined. A huge responsibility falls on any audience when final pitch is granted meaner value than the principles determining that pitch. If the necessity of each note in a whole piece becomes explicable before composition, the eventual tones will minimize sensuality; if carried to extremes the music would lack not only tone but sound—beautiful on paper perhaps, but not so intriguing to listeners.

At first glance the champions appear to have made their own rules, thereby avoiding the real problems of music writing. Actually their devices are neither especially novel nor gratui-

4 Today they're on somewhat better terms, at least the younger practitioners who fuse the three methods.

tous. Advertised as "experimental," atonality nevertheless dates
back fifty years, and the pre-canonic molds into which it is
generally poured are nearly as old as music itself.

The revival of formal chromaticism is less defendable in the
United States today than in Europe. A decade ago American
musical history reached a turning point and refused to turn—
or rather, made a complete about-face. The government encouragement of the thirties and isolation of the early forties
released America from foreign cultural yokes and forced her
to rely on the homemade. Her music began soaring to inde-
pendence. But around 1950, with the renewal of international
highways, reaction set in. Europe reawakened into the past and
took up where she'd left off, notably with the twelve-tone
system, which in America had atrophied. At the cue we aban-
doned a personal path, resuming that of overseas with an
acquiescence misnamed "progressive."

Twelve-tone music and its derivatives are not only historically
but economically more European than American. The rich and
powerful air waves of central Europe provide the main outlet
for all music there. The subsidized radio directors are highly
disposed toward serial music and their plump commissions
extend uniquely to composers of similar disposition. So young
musicians, who like to be heard and always need money, com-
ply by writing the sort of music expected of them. This applies
as well to electronic and chance music. America has no such
subsidies, but she does have electronics, and probably thought
up the music of chance.

Electronic music means the mechanical fabrication of
hitherto unheard sonorities and their formal combination. The
results are remarkably effective. But like jazz effects, these open
new frontiers of scoring rather than composition. Scoring is a
practical craft, not an art. However one classifies electronics,
their invention has high theatrical caliber and sometimes contains the special thrill identified solely with art works. Perhaps

the layman would be more indulgent, the initiate less defiant, if they ceased disputing this expression's validity as music. The definition is less to the point than the effects of organized sound, which can be moving.

Electronic origins go back some forty years to the percussion experiments of Varèse and Cowell. They developed logically with the mechanisms of our age. The outcome is no revolution in language, but one of music's dialects with the syntax still indefinite, the vocabulary small.

The third experimental school is the "farthest out" and best revealed through the person of John Cage, a genius without talent, and leading exponent of an attitude contradicting Ravel's that "in art nothing is left to chance." He also contradicts his serial colleagues who deal with totally predictable situations. Chance music is truly existential: it supposedly eliminates beginnings and ends and retains just the middle, the *Now*. Since Existentialism derives from (and is really as old as) the Zen Buddhism currently in style, it's no wonder the Chinese *Book of Changes* has influenced Cage and his friends whose music is sometimes dictated by a throw of dice. The school's dissenters feel that when all is surprise, nothing is surprise; the unexpected alone cannot make a work. They add that chance elements operate in all artists who forage among semiconscious alternatives. But anyone can throw dice: it requires no taste, no talent, no training.

In Manhattan there is now a Theater of Chance. There has long been painting of chance, poetry of chance, and a vast prose literature of chance which is really what we used to call stream of consciousness. But it all resembles conscious variations on age-old material coordinated by that sense of form inevitable to every art. Despite intentions, it is no chance that one "work of chance" surpasses another.

Composers of chance along with those of serial and electronic methods are, for the moment, the "in" musicians forming a

front against the conservatives. These last-named incline toward
tonality, toward a harmonic texture, a neo-romantic style, and a
neo-classic form. They are not "far out," being neither research-
ers nor innovators. "Conservative" is probably an inappropriate
word, but then so are "conventional" or "conformist." For it is
conventional to be "in"; and since the "ins" are all "far out," being far out is actually conformist. They call themselves the Post
Avant Garde because they're more interested in results than
devices, more involved with sound than procedure, more concerned with being better than with being different. Hence they
are different as they sail over present vogues to a point of
expressive freedom beyond. Indeed, self-expression might be
the chief point in their favor—though it can hardly be considered new.

The conservatives sometimes borrow elements from the experimentalists (though only for expressive purposes, of
course!), while the experimentalists seldom revert to emotive
romanticism. In fact, they can shudder at the very word emotion. Naturally emotion must be controlled by any artist, but
one should let him retain a little to control or his purpose is
defeated. . . . Yet even jazz musicians show signs of scientific
objectivity.

Jazz, chromatico-electronics, and diatonic neo-classicism
signify more than mere trends: far from being radical they are
quite official. Since 1914 little basic change has occurred, only
a categorizing of these three fields. No new forms have been
invented, just new jargons—each one now wholly academic
and encouraged at our better schools.

Possibly music has evolved as far as it will while staying
what is agreed to be music; maybe it now must broaden like
roots rather than heighten like foliage, like space ships away
from mankind. For though mankind's present indifference to
art may be either a cause or effect of that art, the fact remains
that audiences are on the downgrade. The rift between com-

poser and public really began almost three hundred years ago
when music became less of a community affair than a personal
one. (That was when the critic first showed up—to bridge the
gap.) What remains of active listeners is culled mostly from
the scientifically oriented who are unsure of what to expect.
They have diverse estimations of the new.

The commonest is: "I don't know anything about music but
I know what I like." The speaker (who may spend a fortune on
non-objective paintings) unembarrassedly adds that modern
music is a tuneless hoax. His "modern music" then turns out
to be something like *The Firebird*, already two wars old. . . .
Or perhaps he is a partisan of the Different and thinks: "I
know all about music but I don't know what I like, so I can only
admit a taste for the original." He may not see the emperor's
new clothes but fears being proved mistaken, and cries *chef-
d'oeuvre* to any novelty. His recognition is doubtful, since even
time-proven masterpieces don't always carry a label.

Other reactions are from people who know about music and
know what they like. Their opinions are not of chic nor ignorance but of the questioning mind. Some feel that music is a
still-blooming fruition of yesterday. The majority see it in decay
from the refinement of means dominating ends. The pseudo-
science of new music, they say, is less compelling than the
"pure" science it stems from; and anyway music is not a
science but an art. Several object to what they call dehumanized
concentration on form over matter (although dehumanization
is itself a human concept). Some understandably complain of
an artist's increasing withdrawal: the public by definition
resents the private. But while such resentment once was
weighted with curiosity, it now is mated with tedium. The regret
is not that new composition disturbs or shocks but that it bores,
boredom being the last state a work of art should induce.

Composers today are suspiciously articulate: many pass more
time explaining than composing. Their complex solutions must
be clarified to a public that doesn't really want ideas about the

thing but the thing itself. If a recent London critic can be believed, the current state of music presents a variety of solutions in search of a problem, the problem being to find somebody left to listen.

The future's measure of our creative pulse may well prove to be the sciences. They have seduced many an artist (yet cannot afford to be seduced by art). One doesn't criticize a method, just the method's results. Poems and pictures are already retreating from methods of obscurantism. Music, not yet. But then music always lags behind the other arts, and all art lags when the world is in trouble.

In any case, there is little truly new in composition, the language having been complete for about a half-century. Of music being composed the finest isn't worried about novelty-at-any-price. It is worried about expressive innovation. With the standardization of both audiences and composing techniques, individual expressivity seems about the one lasting goal.

The true advance guard is freedom—that of being honest about one's own creative logic on one's own terms. Little such freedom exists when art grants priority to style over content.[5] The liberation will doubtless come, as in the past, through a great man. I, for one, do not yet perceive him among musicians; fresh talent today is busy elsewhere. But let us hope he will arrive before the dwindling need of formal beauty finally vanishes.

Buffalo, October 1960

---

[5] Today the "style" is to consider style and content as one.

VARIATION TWO

Music for the Mouth

to Nell Tangeman (1918–1965)

"She whose songs we loved the best
is voiceless in a sudden night."
—*Elinor Wylie*

"What comes easy is seldom appreciated."
—*Henry Miller*

"Where do you get your facts?"
"I invent them."
—*Peanuts*

3

Writing Songs

Song-writing is a specialty within the general field of musical composition just as the writing of poems, novels, plays, or history is a specialty in the area of literal or verbal interpretation of human experience. In emphasizing songs I will present some general principles which underlie all composition, as well as some practical problems which face the individual composer.

I have chosen song-writing to illustrate a composer's methods for several reasons. Song is one of the briefest musical forms. Its concern with words makes it less "abstract" than other music, therefore more accessible to the non-composer. In song, words are encompassed by a melodic flow of short enough duration for the good listener to feel logically how he is taken from beginning to end. The composer's decisions are fewer and clearer to the layman, and less complex than in systems of development needed for larger and purely instrumental pieces.

Problems of music-making vary from medium to medium and no two composers solve them in the same way. My purpose is not to explain how to write a *great* song; its qualities cannot be ascertained even after it exists because the essence of greatness cannot be verbalized. Nor am I concerned with questions of inspiration. A composer takes inspiration for granted and proceeds directly to perfecting his technique; a facility with his craft is ultimately second nature, so his choices are not always conscious. What I hope to show is a manner by which a song might be written from start to finish. Its future after that is speculative.

For the purpose of this examination I will narrow the definition of song as follows: *A lyric poem of moderate length set to music for single voice with piano.*

A lyric poem is an expression of its author's feelings rather than a narrative of events. A moderate length is up to five minutes. Single voice means the instrument of one human singer. And piano is the instrument with which we are all familiar.

Which comes first, chicken or egg? Words or music? In the world of jazz, lyrics are sometimes concocted specially to synchronize with music already completed. In literature of the formal vocal recital, music always comes second, being a result of the words—a wedding, so to speak, of words and music, in which neither ought dominate the other. A third element of greater magnitude is indicated. This "whole" is a piece of music integrally employing the impetus of words, and differs from a programmatic work that is meant to evoke an image or story without oral recourse.

The composer may force a lyric into the mold of a melody already existing in his notebook and which seemed to be waiting for just these words to come along. In my own working the notebook ideas later used in songs become accompaniment figures above which a tune is imposed. A composer may also have drafted tunes so embryonic they take on entirely new character when joined with words. As a rule, pianistic and vocal ingredients are conceived simultaneously. Today, especially, accompaniment is often composed as a counterpoint equal to the solo line.

The composer's initial job is to find an appropriate poem. The test of this is a poem's final enhancement by music; it is contrariwise inappropriate when both words and music add up to an issue of mutual confusion. One poem may be so intrinsically musical that a vocal setting would be superfluous. Another may be so complex that an addition of music would mystify rather than clarify its meaning.

All words of a song from lyric poetry are ideally understood in a continuing stream; making them comprehensible is the composer's (and ultimately the singer's) chief task. Some songwriters are free in reiterating words and phrases stated only once by the poet. It is uncertain whether such song-writers do this to illuminate the sense, or because they are carried away by their own music and haven't enough words to see them through. A poem *read* aloud with these gratuitous redundancies would not only sound wrong, but lose all of the author's metrical flavor.

A song is not a poem read aloud but something else entirely; music inclines to alter a poet's rhythmic subtlety, no matter the composer's will to prevent it. The sin of duplicating words at discretion is that it retards and cripples the motion intended in verse.

Sung words will almost always be slower than spoken ones, even without repetition; songs last longer than their poems. If the poet is alive he can be consulted about alterations. If he is not, it would seem the more interesting problem is that of making a poem comprehensible without resorting to facile verbal repetition. However, specialized verse forms (such as certain folk songs, nursery rhymes, and jazz improvisation) can lend themselves to arbitrary inner repeating.

A sung poem should be comprehensible without amending the text if declamation and prosody are correct, the tessitura plausible, melodic rise-and-fall natural, and tempo indication comfortable. You may have wondered what these words mean.

Declamation is the effective rhetorical rendition of words with regard to correct emphasis of each word as it relates— sense-wise—to the others. What is called *melodrama* is a procedure of speaking words with systematic accents against musical background. Milhaud, in his *Orestes* cycle, makes hair-raising use of melodramatic declamation: the fury mutters and spits and howls in rhythm with an all-percussion orchestra.

Prosody is the science or art of versification, the synchronizing of musical phrases with the natural movement of speech.

Tessitura refers to that part of the compass in which most of the tones of a melody lie. It should not be confused with *range*—meaning the entire possible gamut of notes a given instrument is capable of performing. A voice's most gracious tessitura is the area of its range in which it performs most graciously.

Excessive concern with these devices will sometimes produce a song so finicky that purely musical values are inhibited. Indifference to word values, using verse solely as an excuse to make music, may result in a song devoid of literary sense. A given poet's style will—where the higher art of song-composition is concerned—refer significantly to the musician's treatment. There is a great gap between the inherent freedom of a folk ballad and the inflexibility of a sestina. Each composer has his approach. The poem's rightness and the success of the resulting song come only with a sense of style and taste in determining the kind of music used with the kind of poem chosen.

These are the principal rules—if you wish—that govern song composition. After a poem has been selected, the effectiveness of its union with sound will result from the composer's judgment in dealing with the words and their ideas.

At this point a digression to examine the poet's attitude about the musicalizing of his verse.

Some poets oppose the process. Tennyson complained:

"These song-writers make me say twice what I have only said once." Valéry stated this same superfluity a bit more prettily: "Hearing verse set to music is like looking at a painting through a stained-glass window." But he personally despaired of poetry's future because of a greater power he felt growing in music.

Walter Pater maintained that "all art aspires to the condition of music." If he were right, poets would long to equal musicians with only verbal tools. Contrasts in language are limited compared to those available in music. Perhaps it is an issue of sour grapes; within their sphere poets surely create an entity, but some feel that the addition of music is gilding the lily.

Others just don't care. Apollinaire's writing was the source for great songs of modern France, yet he was not particularly musical. His attitude was: "If the musicians are amused, let them go ahead, I have no objections!" But he saw no relation between his words and the music.

And the late Paul Eluard was unable to recognize his own verse as realized by Poulenc. Preoccupied with the qualities of human speech, he felt vaguely betrayed by singers. "But since composers have to set something," he would say, "why not me?" He was active in the Surrealist party, which is *a priori* disinterested in music. This disinterest seems to be less the result of repugnance than a disguise of inner fear. (Kafka too was afraid of music.)

Yeats is a tempting poet for composers, but now that he is dead, music editors must apply to his widow for permission. She is said to go into a trance and consult the spirit of her husband with regard to a composer's eligibility. The ghost of Yeats has been known to relent where incompetent musicians are concerned; remarkable settings of his work, however, remain unprinted.

I believe T. S. Eliot allows certain of his poems to be used by all, others by none. Edith Sitwell favors Sir William Walton. Auden is agreeable and seems receptive to most comers; moreover, he is deeply musical. But like many who are well-informed about a trade without practicing it, his observations tend to be impractical or pedantic.

In Old England some composers wrote lyrics for their own songs—like John Dowland and Thomas Campion. In other cases musician and poet alike were commissioned by the court. Purcell fancied the verse of his contemporary Dryden. And everyone knows Gilbert and Sullivan.

Goethe liked his poems set to music but defensively preferred lesser composers; he felt Schubert overpowered his words. Maeterlinck allowed Debussy to use his text of *Pelléas et Mélisande* as an opera, but fell asleep while hearing it.

Colette, who imagined a wonderful libretto for Ravel's *L'Enfant et les Sortilèges* (even the stage directions could be sung!) was overcome by the music: it made her text breathe and shimmer and bloom. She felt—too modestly, I believe— that her words were but a humble foundation upon which a masterpiece was constructed.

Young poets today love having their verse set. Since they have no public anyway (except each other), they hope this unification of the arts will give them prestige through reflected glory. Many are willing to write poems, or even extended librettos, without remuneration, for any composer who asks. But they are inclined to provide material so esoteric that it becomes meaningless when sung.

The modern composer understandably prefers to set poetry by his national contemporaries, but the pickings are slim. Lyric poetry is out of fashion today. As for librettos, a dramatist may have a better sense of music-theater than a poet whose product is by nature fussy, and who seems to forget that what is seen need not be sung about.

Maybe song-writers should amend their notion of what constitutes a proper poem for music-setting. Or perhaps song has grown obsolete. Not infrequently the composer will revert to the Bible, Shakespeare, or romantic schools of the eighteenth and nineteenth centuries to search out texts for his lyrical songs.

Certain American poets, in possible revenge against songwriters, have taken to reciting their works to the accompaniment of improvised jazz. The trouble here is that the poem is an unchanging quantity while this music is never twice the same; the two elements are mutually exclusive. If the poet were consistent he would either request an unalterable backdrop for his narration, or would himself improvise verse to the spontaneous music. Of course, the latter situation would lead to incantation and hence to the Blues—back where it all started!

The Beat Generation is the first literary movement to concern itself seriously with music. But it has achieved nothing in this. The connection is merely a vague endorsement of extra-musical emotions stimulated by the rhythm (or beat) of jazz, and is quite different from an organized union of words with music.

Poets are not always musical, nor even necessarily literary (poetry is about words, not ideas). They are rarely the best judges of the type of music to be used for their verse, although one finds that eminent writers are amenable to word changes a composer might wish to make, while the unestablished or mediocre will not be swerved from details of their original conception.

Song-writing is a collaborative and therefore impure expression. Collaboration implies concession, but concession is, after all, a part of adaptability which in itself is learning. In this sense the self-imposed limitation of the medium is a severe test of technique.

The song-writer writes what he hopes a singer can perform and should be willing to change notes at a singer's suggestion if given a valid reason. The professional poet too might alter a phrase if the composer's request seems rational. Lesser artists, conforming to cliché ideas of integrity, live in ivory towers. Not that a creator should not be idealistic; he can sharpen his craft by keeping an open mind to advice offered by executants who, after all, know more than he about performance. This applies both to poets in relation to composers, and to composers in relation to singing performers.

Before he begins work, a composer would do well to obtain rights for a lyric by applying either to the poet himself or to the publisher. Otherwise the music may be denied hearing and printing. Prior to the advent of copyright laws composers faced no such problem and uninhibitedly indulged their bias for the writings of contemporaries.

Although there may be a scarcity of suitable poetry, the practice of making songs from the work of living writers is desirable. Artists of today, whether they know it or not, have basically more in common with each other than they have with artists of the past. I might add that the music most comprehensible to the people of today is the music of today, because it is penetrated by today.

When he has found a poem, the composer inspects it with an eye toward determining the music's dimensions. The term "song form" is too broad for precise meaning. There are as many forms for a song as there are groups of singable, organized words. Regular lyrical systems exist, such as couplets, quatrains, sonnets, odes, hymns, roundels, even limericks, and also arbitrary sequences which poets invent and order to the nature of their mood.

None of them really fits the so-called ternary A-B-A framework which applies less to vocal than to instrumental music. Or rather, in a general way, it can apply to *all* music in that pieces have beginnings, middles, and end at a point related to the start.

The A-B-A form consists of a primary tune, a secondary tune, and repetition of the primary tune. The commonest version today, our thirty-two-measure pop song, is slightly more complicated: there the first A is repeated twice. This repetition establishes the theme, so that we feel at home with its return from the more transitory B section. Most "popular" music is built on this formula, and some of it—the show tunes of Gershwin, for instance—is unsurpassed in its way. But the music of so-called Art Song takes form from the poem itself, which is seldom versified in the primitive fashion of pop lyrics.

Whatever the poem's design, in one way or another it always dictates the shape of the song. No matter how many liberties the composer takes, it will be the poem itself which provokes these liberties. Meretricious originality is to be avoided at all cost. This might be illustrated by what Hollywood arrangers call Mickey-Mousing; for example, when a brick falls on the protagonist's foot the music goes *ouch!* A composer is not required to write a "lovely" chord on the word "love," or score a bleak low note on the word "death." He seeks to shed light on a meaning of the poem without musico-literary interpretation; he would otherwise be doing what Tennyson deplored: saying twice what the poet says once.

There is obviously no one adaptation of a poem. Different composers have put the selfsame words to different music, each with similar success, each lending both personal poignancy and impact to their understanding of the poem.

There are nevertheless valid unorthodoxies. For instance: a song-writer might have the music play against the words, just as a choreographer has his dancers move against the beat. Dancers can move with extraordinary effect in animated precision to a sustained music with an indefinite meter. The meaning of their motion is nonetheless an evocation of the music, just as in song the meaning of notes is born of words. Although music has a more primal appeal than poetry and is thereby inclined to take over a song, a composer cannot deny that it is the particular expressivity of the given words that provokes the musical mood.

Words provoke the musical mood in a number of essentially mysterious ways. It might be assumed that a song's most logical shape is that which conforms exactly to the shape of the poem. Though it cannot rhyme—as poets understand the word— musical meter can literally illustrate poetic meter: four stanzas of poetry can be imitated by four "stanzas" of identical music. The difference is in the words, which are not the same for each stanza. But a free adaptation is accomplished by ignoring given divisions of a poem and substituting others, or even fashioning a long non-repetitive melody which blends the stanzas into a single current.

On the other hand, a musician may choose free verse and subject it to rigid patterns of tonal repetition, imposing a new dimension extraneous to the music; or he may allow the free verse to carry him along according to its own rules as he himself carried the strict verse in the previous example. Whatever happens, the poem and music will always have a common superstructure.

A composer examines verses with an intention of determining what manner of music will coincide with what words in what section of the poem. He seeks highs and lows, and points of intensity toward which to direct emphasis. Most likely he will first decide upon the musical climax by looking for a group of words that sum up the poet's message, hoping among them to find one with dramatic connotation, and also a vowel that will sound good on a low or high note. Use of a note in extreme vocal registers is the commonest method for producing effective climax in song.

Particular types of voice have a particular tessitura that is more touching than others. We assume the composer is writing for a particular voice. Just as he would know that the soliloquy of a girl in love is not suitable to a bass, nor a warrior's marching tune appropriate for a typical soprano, so he would probably not arrange the most telling moment of his bass line to lie in an upper and strained tessitura, nor allow the high point of the coloratura's song to fall on middle-C.

The climactic note (or phrase) of a song is one that is the result of accumulated tension; contrast is achieved by removing this note from the normal tessitura of speech.

I am not sure that high and low have our implication of tension and release in other cultures, but with Western, vocal music audiences find satisfaction in well-contrived high or low endings, soft or loud endings, endings of contrast, endings that sound difficult (even when they're not). Audiences like all endings: they feel that the virtuoso has run a risk and come out victorious. And they like to be sure when the end has come, so as to know when to clap.

It is no concession to be considerate of public appeal in a final stroke that provides extreme notes for a singer. All music must contain climax. In song it appears when a vocal line arrives at the inevitable point toward which it has been moving. Since a composer feels safer in knowing where he's going, before he begins composition he calculates this point of crisis, insuring the direction of the road which will lead him—both forward and backward—to his overall form. This overall form is what gives contour to melody.

Melody, of course, is the primary ingredient of song: simply say the word and it suggests the human voice! But what is a great melody? Can a musician learn to write one?

Great melodists are not necessarily great composers. Nor is it prerequisite of a composer to be able to make unforgettable tunes. We associate the continuous arching flow that is melody not with Beethoven, Debussy, and Stravinsky, but with Tchaikovsky, Sibelius or Bellini, from whom the well-proportioned long phrase emerges painlessly. Yet the first-named are widely thought to be more "important."

A composer's inborn talent for good tunes probably determines the medium upon which he will concentrate. Those, like

Beethoven, who have difficulty in evolving attractive melodic material to be developed into a work of multiple variations, are likely to center their interest in larger forms where evolution of material is of itself the keynote. Others, like Puccini, who seem disinclined to imagine tunes without words, and whose tunes are born as spacious lines all but complete in themselves, will probably concentrate on vocal mediums. Still others, like Mozart, direct their melodic gifts to every field.

There are all sorts of good melodies, ranging from a four-note motive to extended growths of inexhaustible variety and renewal, yet always related to the seed from which they flowered. These many kinds of melody share in common the gratifying proportions that provide artistic fulfillment. The components of good melody *can* be analyzed from a purely technical standpoint; hence a musician of average ability is capable of inventing one. But that special something that makes it memorable, endows it of mysterious embodiment with power to move us, begs analysis. No one, not even the composer, can tell you much about it.

I noted earlier the importance of words being understood, and proposed that only certain vowel sounds are practical in extreme registers. One vowel sound is practical when it is easier than another for the singer to produce, and so for the hearer to comprehend. For example, "i" is more comfortable high and low than "e." An intelligent composer will not choose the vowel "i" for an extreme note, without good reason, just because it's easy; nor conversely use an impossible "e" in a similar place only because the atmosphere seems to require it.

An offbeat vocal effect can have justification; but the composer has only to try singing it for himself to discover what he imagined dramatic is that, or on the other hand, ineffectual and ridiculous. What is more, he should be able to sing everything he writes no matter how grim his voice sounds. The music we best understand is the music we make for ourselves, and no composer can go far wrong if he estimates his vowels and consonants and prosody and all other attributes of song by letting them come naturally from his own vocal cords while in the act of composing. What he can do, his performer can do; but if he writes only what is theoretically performable, he is in for some jolts.

Setting words with a skill for declamation is said to be a rare gift, yet it is no more than notating words according to the laws of natural speech inflection. Irreproachable declamation is really no more indispensable to song than assigning practical vowels to appropriate notes. A poem, after all, is not "real life"—a song even less so. In this distillation of life, distortions are conceivable when they serve an expressive gesture. If a composer is going to distort the metrical values of a poem he should have good reason for risking loss of verbal comprehension.

The words of Art Song (how I hate that term!) are doubly hard to understand, even when they follow prosodic patterns, because the voice is taken out of normal speaking range. In jazz and folk songs, words are understood without effort, for these tunes are generally built within the limits of an octave which the singer transposes to his own speech range—and then emits through a microphone.

In verse as in the prose of speech phrases have an innate rise and fall which is rendered in the same way by most readers. In music, regular fidelity to this rise and fall makes for monotony, yet occasional consideration of it can be pertinent. The composer may disregard the effects of natural language for musical reasons, and such departures are part of the act of composition.

Now the question of accompaniment. Accompanists dislike the word and call themselves pianists. They feel that the best songs are a supple give-and-take between instruments of equal worth, and that an insensitive pianist will sabotage the greatest vocalist.

Accompaniment is classically a regulated pattern over which a voice moves. This is as true of, say, Schubert's songs as of his piano sonatas wherein the voice is not human. Accompaniment has evolved since the troubadours sang their tunes above a simple strumming, and instrumental sounds that used merely to sustain a voice are often now on equal terms with it, weaving in and out of, sometimes overwhelming, the vocal line. Piano parts of Debussy's late songs are virtuoso pieces; voice and keyboard have independent developments indicating a chamber duet rather than what we normally think of as a song.

Accompaniment reduced to its lowest terms does not, however, exist as a piece in itself, though a good vocal part retains its urgency even when performed alone. The composer may imagine that he conceives a work for voice *and* piano, but under our limited definition of song, it is music for voice *with* piano.

In the end, composition is choice, nothing more: choosing the right note to be sounded with the right tone in the right place at the right time, each choice presenting alternative decisions, other possibilities. But choices are not always conscious. I have mentioned inspiration as a presupposed faculty; and, when the tools of craft are well in hand, awareness of them has less importance than what they produce.

The majority of song-composers write quickly: with the poem they have something to start with, the skeleton exists. If the composer has a good day this skeleton will acquire an inevitable flesh. He does not know the origin of this flesh, nor is he especially aware of its sequential growth.

His very first efforts doubtless came from sheer instinct without practical knowledge of the voice (except that which sang within him), or of musical form (except that which the poem seemed to indicate). Such songs can be quite good indeed, but this goodness troubles an untrained composer when he isn't sure why it is good. Probing the nature of song by studying formal vocal devices found in other people's music will not inhibit but release his ability. He will still write for the same "inspired" reasons, but with the assurance of an intervening knowledge without which he would have stood still.

Since the so-called born song-writer's early pieces have usually worked by instinct, he spends the rest of his life attempting to make tangible the fortunate formulas which originally appeared without his calling them. His young songs came to life, as it were, from the exuberance of first love. First love is unexpected revelation which seldom reoccurs except to saints and artists.

Song-makers are so often reproached for not writing a "grateful" vocal line, or for misrepresenting a text, that they can assume the listeners do not hear as they do. There are as many reactions to music as there are people to hear it. The composer desires to bridge the gap between private conception and public reception. He does so by learning a recipe of indispensable ingredients. Later, if he is still around, he does it by trying to teach his interpreter to hear as he hears.

I have suggested that certain principles of song-writing become obsessive and distorted. These distortions are successful when their purpose is not aesthetically gratuitous. The church music of Palestrina and his colleagues was less bound to words as literature than to their use for evoking the glory of God through choral counterpoint. A single syllable was strung out to such length that it could not be understood as having literal connotation. It was employed for its musical, and therefore religious, sound.

A modern example which gives a total interpretation of text at the expense of individual phrase comprehension, is the setting by Boulez of René Char's *Le marteau sans Maître*. The

word values are so purposely deranged and the vocality so unnatural that the most agile enunciation could never project a
literal sense. Boulez's intention was to interpret the poet, not
the poem. He portrayed, in his way, a feeling for the author,
using the words as a frame around his sound.

The opposite intention can be found in Thomson's setting of
Gertrude Stein. The speech values are so exact, the melodies so
"normal," the accompaniment so functional, that there is no
question of each word being heard with the significance given
by the poet. Or Satie, whose music on the prose of Plato allowed
each syllable an ease of talk, brightened only by a discreet
simultaneous French commentary on the old Greek.

Any words can be turned into song if the composer's aim is
as sure as the text's. Celius Dougherty made a riotous encore
out of the definition of Love as found in the dictionary.

Lou Harrison wrote a disturbingly effective essay on chloro-
phyll in Esperanto, then set it for eight baritones and orchestra.
John Cage took a prose extract from *Finnegan's Wake* and
arranged it gorgeously for soprano on just three notes, accompanied by hand-tapping on all parts of the piano save the keyboard. Milhaud used words from a flower catalogue, and Bern-
stein from a recipe book for charming cycles.

The writer of songs—by way of recapitulation—is a category
of composer who can't always express himself on broader instrumental terrains, any more than a symphonist can necessarily make the lone lyric page a totality. Nor can he work
without what he feels to be appropriate poetry, the test for
which lies in his ability to add a fresh dimension by way of
music (can he clarify a poem to an audience through a singer?).

Song is of greater magnitude than either text or music alone.
The composer is concerned with words only insofar as they
are related to music. Sometimes his comprehension of a poem
is not fully realized until after he has completed the fusion.

Speaking for myself, the only poems I've ever really "understood" are those I've put to music. This understanding resembles that of the astronomer for whom stars change their meaning as he approaches.

When the composer has decided upon a poem he should inquire as to whether it is in public domain or still subject to copyright laws.[1] He then examines the general tone of the text, sensibly, stanzaically, metrically. His music will move either with or against the normal flow of the poem according to what permits the most sensitive rendition. He takes care not to obscure comprehension of the words, but to illuminate them with regard to the dictates of rise and fall, of prosody and declamation, and of vowel and consonant properties.

The overall nature of the text determines the contour of melody. Extreme points of a song's melody are, in turn, deter-

---

[1] Blushingly, may I append an appropriate morality-anecdote as antidote to the forgoing pedantry? . . . In 1948 I composed a setting of Edith Sitwell's *Youth With the Red-Gold Hair*. My publisher said: "Fine. Get the poet's o.k. and we'll print the song." I'd hitherto musicalized any words that appealed to me; my few songs already published had been to verse in Public Domain, i.e. no longer controlled by International Copyright laws. It hadn't occurred to me that living poets might have opinions —much less objections—about having songs made on their work. . . . I mailed a genteel request to Sitwell, and received no reply. After four months I wrote again, —again no reply. In France a year later I stated the case personally to Satchervell Sitwell and to Stephen Spender who, after hearing the music, promised to intercede. Still no answer. Once more I wrote. Silence. Eventually I received from the Sitwell editors a note to the effect that Walton was the only composer the lady favored, but that if I could persuade him to make an exception in my case, they might reconsider. Walton's secretary answered me from Ischia stating that the master was deep in *Troilus & Cressida*, but if I would write again in six months, etc. I wrote again in six months, and so did my publisher. No reply. Finally, exasperated, four years after my first enquiry, I sent off a letter of such ugly rebuke that Braziller's lawyer will not permit its reproduction here. Suffice that I demanded a simple yes or no. By return mail the attorneys responded: ". . . you complain that she has ignored your request to be allowed to use a poem of hers of which you had in fact made use before you asked. Dr. Sitwell receives a constant stream of requests from unknown persons who wish to hitch their wagons to her star and has in self defense been forced to a policy of ignoring them. . . ."

mined not only by an inherent sense of "rightness" but also by
knowledge of the most "telling" registers of the vocal range
for which it's written.

Behind this melody occurs an accompaniment as a subsidiary
part of song, though recently it has come to have almost equal
value with the solo voice.

Any competent craftsman can fabricate an impeccable song
in which every note is justified by some sort of musico-prosodic
logic. One composer will undertake the writing slowly, with
controlled manipulation not requiring "inspiration" (which
comes in irregular spurts anyway). Another will produce his
song in a fever of impulse with music spilling out all at once;
in a single sitting, innately aware of his technical resources, he
knits the sundry components of words and music into a coherent whole.

A professional has only a subconscious inkling of his working
methods once they are ingrained. He is in the happy position of
not being obliged to give himself an explanation for his individual choices if their sum total seems logical. It is for the theorist
to inquire later into the reasons of choice; they may not necessarily jibe with those of the composer who may even have forgotten them.

No system guarantees a great song, although a well-trained
musician may turn out a flawless one by academic standards.
The artist's hand is not wingèd every day. The magic touch
cannot be willed. But without it a writer of songs—whether he
has a dazzling technique, an intelligent conviction of "what
should be," even an unquenchable inspiration—will deliver a
stillborn imitation. A flawless song becomes great when it contains the breath of life.

Summer 1959

4

Anatomy of Two Songs

New structures can be made from the same
blocks, but the blocks are all quite ready from
childhood on. Only in childhood are we destined
to collect them and pick them up.—*Mahler*

During November of 1949 in Morocco I kept a Journal of Songs
wherein I dissected, after the fact, recollections about the
making of a dozen vocal works. The following examples pertain
to pieces from my student days, three years previous.

Spring and Fall

Clearly this song owes its existence to Monteverdi's madrigal
Amor. Why apologize? For centuries good friends have been
exchanging ground basses (there's not an original plot in all
Shakespeare); I simply took this one without asking.

It was composed for Christmas 1946 to delight my sister
Rosemary (unmarried at the time), because Hopkins had sub-
titled his poem "To a young child." But the dedication on the
printed music is for Eva Gauthier, easily seventy, because. . .

That printed music is in the key of one sharp. Conceived
by me in the key of four flats, it was transposed by the publisher
so that it would sell better. Indeed, only a very pure tenor could

start "Margaret" and "Come" on so quiet a high G! In four flats then, the opening figure was an impulse from something by a colleague about a nun. I changed the order of notes, and so rendered them invisible. Where the overall melody came from I don't know: it now looks (and sounds) woven improvisationally from fluid threads around the solid ostinato. Probably I wrote first the music to the final verse—"It is Margaret you mourn for"—and proceeded backwards. The poem I had known vaguely for ten years (since the time Norris Embry declaimed it into a hear-your-voice-back machine at Chicago's Museum of Science and Industry), but decided to musicalize it only in the summer of '46 when Sarah Cunningham sang me her version which I needed to improve upon.

Good Guy Ferrand, always astute, has pointed out the note-for-note resemblance between the melodic line "This is our Lordly Hudson," and the piano part of *Spring and Fall* against the words ". . . same. Nor mouth had, no nor mind, expressed. . ." I'd never noticed. But since I pilfered only myself, there is no call for shame.

None of the rests should be literal. A lot of pedal to avoid jerkiness. The "Ah!" must be slightly gasped. "Ghost-guessed" should be practiced two hundred times. Singing is easy.

On a Singing Girl

This is one of my few songs written as a temporary emotional release. Composing as a craft can be a permanent release—but not emotionally, only technically: it keeps you busy.

I was sitting, waiting, exhausted, in the lobby of Juilliard. A girl I know came up to say that our mutual friend Teru Osato had only four months to live. Under my arm was a book of American poems. I whispered to myself: why not write a song while waiting.

Elinor Wylie had made a rhymed transliteration from the Greek of an epitaph for a musical slave girl who had died young. (Oh, the connection with Teru hadn't struck me, really, until now.) I wrote out the vocal line right there on my lap, over-tailoring the prosody as was then my obsession.

So the voice was complete in itself, though I had no idea of how the accompaniment would go until I reached home that evening. I'd learned that if a vocal line is conceived alone it will probably take on the rambling curves of nature rather than the artificial curves—square curves, you might say—of folk song; for coherence, a systematized accompaniment is indicated. (Contrariwise, sometimes in our piano improvisations we hit upon a figuration so pretty that any silly tune can be successfully superimposed.)

I needed square curves. Having just come to know Paul Bowles' *David*, I decided to disguise some of the piano part of that into a background design. Such conscious plagiarism is safe, remorse leads us to sabotage innovators, we sign our names. Who is the wiser? Certainly not Paul. Artists—by definition innocent—don't steal. But they do borrow without giving back.

This song, like most of mine, was made in a couple of hours. Nobody sings it much because it reacts like sandpaper on flayed fingertips. The closing words, "dust be light," were originally an octave higher. Povla Frijsh lowered them to their now-inevitable position. Always listen to singers, even when you can't see them shrieking back there in the brain.

For the record I've mentioned dear Teru, but the music is dedicated to Danny Pinkham because he and I were the only ones writing songs in those days. Singing is difficult.

5

Song and Singer

Songs and song recitals of our time have become trivial objects
to almost everyone: to composer and manager, publisher and
public alike. Singers themselves are still very much around, but
have turned into a salable commodity. Big Business, in shelving
the "miniature," has decalcified the performer's repertory and
vulgarized his public image—because money is not carried on
wings of song. When art falls to the low point of a curve as it
has today, its smallest treasures are the first to break from the
weight of false standards. Prizes for bad symphonies are higher
than for good songs, although lengthy pieces make the average
listener more uneasy than shorter ones. Most painting collectors
prefer big canvases because they're worth more; and if large
pictures delight while long music bores, the layman's criteria
are nonetheless based (in art as in cigarettes) on size before
quality. Musically those criteria are imposed by impressarios
who disqualify voice recitals except for an occasional prestige
venture. A few song-writers and concert-singers still specialize,
of course, though they are not in demand. But their specialty
was once an invulnerable art whose periods of perfection coin-
cided with the peaks of musical history.

The history of music is the history of song, since all music
evolves from vocal expression; the Neanderthal probably sang

his worship of nature before thinking of any other artistic utterance. Yet music is frequently claimed to have flowered last of the arts. Naturally its group expression, its instruments are prehistorical, and Grecian modes and flutes and zithers were not invented yesterday. Still, comparatively speaking, music as the formal tool of a single author *is* from yesterday.

One explanation lies in ancient man's exclusion of psychic exploration from the avowable pleasures of his artistic soul. His pyramids and sphinxes emerged from a balance between the human ideal and the tangible world, while music exploits effects without cause—which is why its power is as obscure as dreams. With the rise of Judeo-Christian culture, psychological rather than logical investigation was stressed. And so creative music, in keeping with the times, grew less concerned with clear-cut ideas. Words, of course, are clear-cut and logical, and all songs have words. In fact, most Western music until modern times was fundamentally vocal—as though ancient man scented danger from afar, and foreseeing our hysteria felt obliged to link his abstract sound to the un-elusive verb. "What ancient man did create," says the poet Valéry, who advanced the above notions, "is nothing next to what he smothered within himself. If poetry attained full realization millenniums before music, the cause was its address to people who had no need of intense physical reaction in their enjoyment of art." I leave to others an enlargement of this theory. Whatever its time relation to the fellow arts, music's beginnings in any civilization are vocal.

Primitives gradually find melody by combining phrases which exaggerate the rise and fall of speech. Vocal contours depend on language and eventually give music a discernible national character. Since vocal music is the source of non-vocal music, speech inflection is the direct basis of all music of all cultures. And since music resembles the speech of a nation, it also resembles the people. People, therefore, resemble their music. Their religious beliefs (which are the origins of song) grow

from fear of nature into praise of it, and hence into the
melodized speech of tribal incantations which finally crystallize
as highly organized chant.

Later Christian liturgy is not far from its Oriental predecessors. The pagan or folk music of the Dark Ages accompanied
systematic bodily movement, not only of dance but of practical
chores like spinning and chopping; hence regular meter. The
religious or art version was reaction against such bodily movement and resulted in the melisma of Gregorian chant; hence
irregular meter.[1]

Although medieval church music underwent meager development, the laity produced a race of nomadic recitalists called
minstrels and troubadours. In the early 1300's they were domes-
ticated (at least in Germany) into Mastersingers and organized
guilds where apprentices learned the trade (not the "art") of
song.

The Renaissance moved singing into even more secular routes,
inventing the madrigal and eventually the single vocal
line with instrumental accompaniment, a direct ancestor of
modern song. This was perfected in Italy by Monteverdi and
the elder Scarlatti, but declined around 1725 by becoming a
mere frame around vocal gymnastics.

In England, Henry Purcell revitalized the art with a poignant
skill unequaled anywhere, while in Germany of the next century,
a literary flowering occurred attended by a corresponding advance in lyric music. The advance reached a climax most cen-
trally in Franz Schubert, followed (as climaxes must be) by a
rapid descent.

The history of music must not be considered an unbroken
flow toward ultimate perfection. A chant of Gregory, a mass of
Machaut, a motet of Gesualdo, a cantata of Bach or a lied of
Schumann are each invariably a masterpiece—and irreplace-

---

[1] Irregular meter *and* a slower tempo, because of echoing cathedrals.

able. Each is a high note in music's story whose high notes have most usually been heard in the human voice.

After Schubert, then, another dark age awaited song. The darkness, to be sure, was occasionally shot with sunlight, for one cannot dismiss the vocal talents of Brahms or Wolf, of Ravel and Debussy. But the tendency was toward total eclipse as demonstrated by the punity and near obsolescence of recent literature for the human voice. Ours is an instrumental age in every way.

And there, in a nutshell, is song's history.

What kind of people are those who sing?

Since Mozart's day prima donnas have been noted for their extravagant temperaments, for all we love in the legend of theater. Yet I can only judge from those around me who mostly seem loyal colleagues, hard workers, and early risers.

Their body is their instrument, so singers require more steady health than other performers. The majority pamper themselves but have generous outgoing natures. They like to eat, drink, laugh, scream, and kiss; they express emotion orally because they enjoy singing. When romance or digestion go wrong, these things said to stimulate creators depress singers, and the tension shows immediately to their public. So they keep themselves the most normal of artists.

At present they capitalize on normality to a monotonous degree. Latter-day divas are said to have followed fabulous conventions expected of them, and their wild self-indulgence served also as vocal expression. The acting of Jeritza, for example, was as brilliant in daily life as on the stage. With the exception of Maria Callas, few retain a semblance of fiery tradition, though Europeans are still more theatrical than Americans. Even in movie stars we admire homey humor before mysterious dynamism. The dynamic singer is vanishing as music becomes less a ceremony than an industrialized game.

Commercial spectacle, in replacing intimate ceremony, has all but killed the small recital both here and abroad. And record catalogues feature about 75 per cent fewer songs than before the war. The public is after bigger game: it wants a voice backed by the sonorous gloss of orchestras and the visual sheen of décors. A singer who can still attract the public to his piano-vocal concerts does so uniquely through an established opera reputation. Usually the recital contains as many arias as songs.

The upshot is that American vocal training accentuates opera repertory nearly to the exclusion of any other. For only in opera (if anywhere) will fortune fall to the lucky aspirant. And so he learns every language—except his own. In this country of specialization, the sole area of general practice is that of vocal literature. If in Europe, where general practitioners prevail, a singer still masters his native tongue first and foremost, our students seem to prefer bad singing in languages they don't speak to good singing in their own. The excuse is that English is ungrateful—but only because the pitfalls are clearer. A vast collection of masterful English songs exists from Purcell and Handel to Britten and Chanler. The only thing bad about English as a vocal medium is bad English.

Too many virtuosos lack curiosity about repertory other than for their own instrument, and singers lead the group. Curiosity may be less expedient than flair to great performance, but *some* intellect would aid in overall musicianship. Our singers are not so untutored as they once were (doubtless because of mechanical exigencies in all fields), yet they remain the least literate of musicians because of their medium's accessibility which offers them a less literate audience. Song is the most natural musical expression. Certainly our best jazz vocalists perform through sheer instinct, though their instrumentalists now are mostly conservatory graduates. If the jazz singer lacerates English prosody and ignores classical breath control, he nevertheless (or rather, she—for the greatest are women), *she* nevertheless works according to a long tradition and her every word is crystal clear.[2] But the recitalist has forgotten traditions —not of singing, but of song.

Song has always bridged the gap between poetry and speech by combining two effects like a double exposure. Song is sound —a sound of greater magnitude than its separate components. Of course the sound of music—as opposed to rustling leaves or words of love—is sensual only secondarily. First it must make sense. Since composers today are less involved with sound itself than its means of production, their training in song is not much happier than the singers'. After the war, just as most authors eschewed the opulence of words, our composers lost the luster of notes, even in big forms. And only a handful of poets and musicians still concern themselves with vocal miniatures as did Schubert and Duparc, Burns and Yeats.

The scholastic trend encourages manipulation of massive structures, so young composers now have masterpiece complexes. Masterpieces are supposed to be long, yet one-page songs can indicate talent as effectively as interminable quartets. And all musical expression (if it is to have an effect as music) is basically a sung expression, whether it be a Stephen Foster tune or an electronic construction. He who composes graciously for any instrument need not be a performer, but must have imagination to sing within himself not only his songs but his symphonies.

The imagination of vocal composition has withered. The same fistful of song-writers existing twenty years ago still persists, but seems clenched tighter than ever. Younger men are not intrigued by word-setting, and when they employ the human voice it is less for verbal expression than for instrumental effect. That effect is shunned by most singers whose instruction has not even begun to explore the non-vibrato tone production which modern vocal music calls for. The singer and

[2] I was referring to any vocalist from Billie Holiday to Nina Simone or even Sinatra, but not to Bob Dylan or The Supremes. (N.R., 1966)

composer work as much at cross-purposes as do composer and audience. And all three seem to have renounced that sense of just plain dazzle from Rossini's time.

The art of serious music is not learned through education alone, of course, but through a sixth sense. Nor again is it an entertainment; it requires concentration, and concentration can be dull at times. But among other things music is fun (or should be) and is not all just scholarly sound.[3]

The ceremony may be seen as well as heard. Stravinsky has organized works for their visible as well as their sonorous aspects. Presumably he does so to reinforce attention on the composition (since closed eyes make for wandering minds), although the ritual of music—from tribal dances to the Catholic Mass—has always involved the visual.

This is especially true as regards singers who, for better or worse, are indispensible to the art of song. They have even more need of stage presence than other executants since they can't beguile you with an instrument other than their own person. The greatest vocalists aren't necessarily the greatest performers, and conversely the most compelling ones don't always make the prettiest noises. When performance and sound are combined in a glamour build-up today as in, say, the case of Eileen Farrell, it means that she is a faithful wife who washes dishes like everyone else while producing sounds that nobody else can produce.

But with all the artless hominess of today's performers (or rather their managers), every good one, despite himself, retains an extra-musical style: from his entrance on the platform to his moment of attack, he is an actor presenting himself, a professional personality who at home may be dull as dish water. Personality is manifest, for example, through Lily Pons's demureness, through Bernac's precision, Callas's bravura, Flag-

---

[3] Entertainment confirms rather than challenges.

stadt's "no nonsense" style, Tourel's illusion of beauty, Della
Casa's true beauty, Siepi's virility, and so forth. As for Americans like Roberta Peters or Theodore Uppman, they accentuate
the kid-next-door approach. Involuntary or studied, all are
showmen. Their audience is reassured when the musical movement arrives because they know what they're doing and how
to do it. Only when showmanship dominates do they become
caricatures like Anna Russell or Liberace.

That magnetism is the executant's artistic projection of a
driving interest; stage comportment is an over-extension of his
character. Such excitement, however, cannot be taught, and its
absence explains why many of our more-than-capable students
just never make the grade. Either they are too stable, or too
dull, or too intelligent, or too sure of themselves.

No virtuosos are sure of themselves, and most are afflicted by
stage fright. Their electricity comes from the sense of risk being
run. The possibility of a ceremony's getting out of hand (as at
a bullfight) spellbinds the spectators. They may be acquainted
with the ritual's climax, but only the virtuoso can lead them to
it for only he knows how to get there, and he may never arrive.
Nothing is sure until complete. The interpreter's voyage exists
in time so he is prey to more perils than the creator. Sometimes
he quite literally dies *en route*. His is not the reason why. The
difference between skillful amateurs and magic professionals
lies less in their understanding than in nervous feeling. The
term "understanding" is vague anyway when applied to art.
Complete understanding is no more a requisite of musical performers than of actors. The actor who overdoes his investigation
of a playwright's motives turns out to be a director, a critic, or a
ham. Great works possess too many levels of diagnosis for one
person to ascertain *and* interpret simultaneously. The performer's job is to project, not analyze. Analysis is for the
musicologist and the composer, and even the composer (if
alive) is dumfounded by the layers of "meaning" a musicologist
may reveal in his composition.

The public, of course, pays for performance more than for what is performed—so the performer capitalizes on that glamour of his. Which is why composers so often resent interpreters. The gratuitously brilliant interpretation naturally sabotages composition as often as the inept one. But occasionally I wonder if truly excellent performance cannot do the same. In such a case does the music itself thrill, or the person's manner of playing it? Qualities of *vocally* performed music are particularly hard to judge. The sense of song is expressed through words, and words have precise meaning no matter how well or badly uttered. Even the wisest have difficulty divorcing themselves from performance since the head finds less use for music than the body. Saint Augustine, after desperate avoidance of the physical, could finally proclaim: "I am moved not with the singing, but with the thing sung." Yet how can we tell the dancer from the dance? And especially where the human voice is involved, anyone has trouble disentangling the sound from what is sounded; for here is the most emotional of instruments which all others seek to emulate.

That emotional ingredient is why so many people shy away from a voice recital. They call it boring really because it strikes home, because they too can sing (in their way) and so can identify, and identification—as Gertrude Stein said—makes you "feel funny." But the funny feeling is a step toward appreciation and can be taken most easily through vocal music. One only regrets that today, with expanding audiences, we are persuaded to identify with the common. Songs, rather than transcending ordinary sentiments, now descend to reaffirm and justify them.

If the tune on paper were questioned, how would it answer? That "heard melodies are sweet but those unheard are sweeter"? For such melodies when brought to life sound far from the composer's first conception. Music lasts by itself and cares not who composed it; nor can music recall the thousand anonymous fingers and mouths which tamper with it, beautifully or badly.

Charles Ives, our musical Grandma Moses, once wrote that his songs had not been made for money, nor fame, nor love, nor kindling; in fact he had not composed them at all but merely cleaned house and proudly hung what was left on a clothesline for the neighbors to see. He explained his pleasure in contriving that which could never be sung. "After all," said he, "a song has a few rights the same as other ordinary citizens. . . If it happens to feel like trying to fly where humans cannot fly, to sing what cannot be sung, to walk in a cave on all fours, or to tighten up its girth in blind hope and faith, and try to scale mountains which are not—who shall stop it? In short, must a song always be a song?"

Buffalo, 1960

VARIATION THREE

Music for the Ear and the Heart

to John Marshall (1920–1966)

"What if some little pain the passage have,
That makes frail flesh to fear the bitter wave?
Is not short pain well home, that brings long ease,
And lays the soul to sleep in quiet grave?
Sleep after toil, port after stormy seas,
Ease after war, death after life doth greatly please."
—*Spenser*

"If I cannot work well then have I the right to eat?"
—*Ned Rorem's Diary*

6

Listening and Hearing

"The ideal listener is one who applauds vigorously."
—*Virgil Thomson*

"What is the answer?" asked Gertrude Stein on her deathbed. There was silence. "Well, then what is the question?"—and she died.

The question, of course, has always been on the universal source and aim. It never changes. But history has provided ten thousand solutions through theology and science whose responses raise other questions; they are forever evolving, never complete. Alone the work of art satisfies, for its question and answer are mutually inclusive and form the one finished thing that exists.

Answers have less value than questions: we can learn them by rote. But curiosity indicates imagination, and imagination represents the first step toward good listening which will result in a comprehensibly musical reply—irrelevant to logic or moral persuasion.

Listening is easy. But true ease, like anything worthwhile, may be hard to cultivate. We hear all the time, even in sleep, though we don't always listen to what we hear. In music, as in living, fragments of question and answer might try the door of our consciousness, then pass unknown and leave us ignorant of what we've missed. Few people develop their capacity for per-

74   Music for the Ear and the Heart

ceiving what is always around; most ears follow a line of least resistance that allows only pleasant passive hearing. Active listening provokes reaction which is not always pleasant, for pleasure is the target of entertainment—a side issue of great music as of great crucifixions.

Since the larger public is passive, it might be desirable to cultivate a listening potential. But too much music is around today. Concentration grows implausible when accompanied by the unsolicited bombardment of Muzak wherever we go. Answers are there, but increasingly disguised by accumulation of rubble. Saturation desensitizes selection, and one cannot distinguish, or even knowingly hear. From self-protection we stop responding actively or passively. Or we stay home with our "serious" recordings which used to be a good proving ground but now demonstrate an obsession quite removed from the living core of art. Omnipresence of music derives not from love of sound but from fear of silence. Sound has no meaning except in relation to silence. Ours is a century of racket—in all senses of the word. So when we finally come to the concert hall our reactivity is dead and the program goes in one ear and out the other.

Not that concerts make an ideal setting. They are a fairly recent addition to audience passivity. Hearing music for its own sake did not occur before the 1700's when it was a joint proposition between composer and performer and hearer, happening at home or at church. Music was either made by oneself or heard as a dedication to God's glory. The décor of discovery is significant: we may be more moved by a new piece in unexpected surroundings than in standard presentation. Solitary confinement inspires more propitious appreciation than the communal museum-jail.[1]

[1] Having first heard Hindemith's Trombone Sonata with a temperature of 103°, I found it a masterpiece. Bartók's Bluebeard under mescaline was doubtful (but then so is all music). My first Piano Sonata (1948) might have turned out quite otherwise if I hadn't had chicken pox while composing it.

In America from 1925 to 1950 jazz fired the young to song and dance and jam sessions which again made them into dynamic contributors. Though not worshiping a special deity they were spontaneously reacting. But now jazz devotees (like concert publics) have renounced physical response and sit in "cool" absorption of their age's hysteria.[2]

Some people say they don't understand music but love it—or they know all about it except what they like—or they haven't learned to appreciate! Despite education we only listen to what we want to hear. Without formal coaching many perceive the maximum subtleties in jazz because it is of their time; they need not work at love. The attraction may be foreign to their parents, who had effortlessly digested the sonorous folkways of *their* heyday. A fashionable fallacy, in our passive age of the large audience, is that those elite communities of the past possessed deeper musicality by virtue of participation. Practical knowledge is urgent to creation but not to comprehension. Sensitivity alone arrives at an estimate of artistic worth. Love is sometimes wise to ignore rules, for technique may distract from effect. We can read with deep fascination of Oedipus or Burma without budging in time or space—without committing murder or building roads.

As for those who feel left out: why, after all, must everyone like music? That they are missing something is just the lover's opinion. Certain fine men simply don't need it, which doesn't signify a profound lack: they merely have other criteria and are honest about them. For that matter, there exists a probable boredom in most audiences most of the time with most music, especially the classics. However, they don't resent the classics because they are used to them and only *hear* them. Modern music usually impels listening, hence reaction. Most people hate to react—though nothing is more wholesome.

---

2 We aren't allowed to dance to Ornette Coleman, but we do now to Rock. The weeks slide by like a funeral procession, but generations pass like a snowstorm.

With artistic benefits and disadvantages of historic change there remain the same inherent levels of listening. But today for the first time civilization offers a minor role to art: the need is replaced by the romance of the atom. Artists have reached a sort of impasse. Artistic distribution and consumption, on the other hand, are more avid than ever, though not very constructive. From the composer's viewpoint the impression is that, whatever the world's state, logical musical education should begin with works of the present as it always did in the past.

Music most comprehensible to people of today is music of today because it is penetrated by today, and literally no one can fail to perceive this on some level. I find it harder to identify with a Haydn sonata than with any modern score: I have a feeling for what my colleagues want to say. Today's music may be difficult because it is alive, and life is difficult. But this very difficulty talks to us even when we don't like what it says, whereas the classics approach us with the pacifying inactivity of corpses. We can only know the past through modern interpretations which change every day. The motionless unknown is judged by the fluid known.

I am not implying that Haydn's value has diminished, simply that we will never hear him with the ears of his time: ours are filled with intervening centuries of sound which Haydn ignored.

The average concert provides scant exposure to the contemporary. Impresarios know that familiarity does not breed contempt, but only more familiarity. They sell the public what they suppose it wants: the "classical" repertory. The concert public has come to associate all music with this music. An overdose of the familiar is a drug dripping the danger of security which in art means being invulnerable. Those who interrogate the unforeseen are truly alive. Familiarity with the classics appears to justify evasion of the new. The classics only seem more comprehensible because they are heard oftener; in reality they are as removed as the communal belief in God which produced Renaissance art. We perceive such art with a far different aesthetic from that of the people to whom it demonstrated a way of life.

Resentment of the new, then, rises from forced dissociation with the old. Yet our own composers, those of whom we should be proud, cannot reiterate. Expression today is more private than the mass celebration of God. Even the elevating powers of the past were less in theme than in treatment. Subject matter is never important—anyone can still praise the heavens if he wants to. Twisted wires, twisted toes, or twisted lives have the same skeletal connotations now as before, but are made timely flesh by Calder, Balanchine, or Albee. An understanding of these treatments is latent, and emerges when the public frees itself from yesterday, not in erasing it, but in judging today by today's standards. The truths of the past are the clichés of the present. Periods of time will always be interactive whatever we decide, as Eliot pointed out when: "Some one once said: 'the dead writers are remote from us because we know so much more than they did.' Precisely, and they are what we know. . ."

If casual hearing is numbed by Muzak, and adventurous listening stifled by average concerts, where, then, do we find our new music and the peace to indulge in it? We can avoid Muzak in the silence of our home, then fill the silence with recordings of our choice. I have suggested that records, though an evasion of the miracle of accident, do supply a proving ground. If the average music lover lacks joys of even a hundred years ago when he himself played chamber music, today, nonetheless, he has access to a much larger repertory on disks; also the advantage of immediate rehearing, prerequisite to familiarity with the new. The majority of hi-fi enthusiasts, however, restrict their collection to the safe music of the usual concert. A safe work is one that tradition has frozen into a masterpiece relieving us of our own decisions. Stereo addicts are frequently more concerned with the techniques of production than in the music produced. The most vociferous record public is, of course, made up of opera fans who are occupied first with a singer's reputation, second with voice production, third with the story, and last but not most with the music. Music itself seems more sport than art, and the vast audience resembles that of a tennis match: heads move in hypnotic unison from left to right to left as a high-C flies over the net to be whammed back by a rival coloratura. But for the exceptional listener—he with questions—records serve as introduction to unusual music, just as concerts introduce items with which he may grow more familiar through disks.

For not all concerts are "average," and even the average occasionally come up with something interesting. Concerts and records are the musical outlets of our time, and are less to be merely tolerated than put to good use. How shall we use them?

If acceptance of the classics has come through familiarity, the same will be true with our own music. Still, appreciation results from repetition only when we listen. To know a piece one must be on friendly terms with it. The structural elements of one language cannot be transferred to another. Thought produces grammar, and different peoples think differently. We don't understand a Frenchman, or even his culture, unless we have some knowledge of his spoken tongue. The knowledge brightens less through study than through exposure.

Exposure to music is active submission, though not always on subjective planes. Only superficially will it soothe the savage breast. Aaron Copland once caused a stir by stating he never cried when hearing music. He explained that while theatergoers may weep easily because of immediate human identification, the gifted listener only lends himself to music's power: "he gets both the 'event' and the idealization of the 'event' . . . even though the music keeps its 'physical distance.'"

Good music that summons no tears doesn't mean we are unmoved; the movement takes us away from (rather than into) ourself. We are removed. If we do weep at a popular tune, that is because it beckons us into ourself, reminds us of an extra-musical past of situations which never return but which we hope to revive in the present. The "memories" are actually revised images existing in the present but associated with circumstances under which the tune was first heard. The images have nothing to do with the music, the past does not exist. Yet in such reveries many of us absorb music, osmosis-wise, involving the ego rather than abandoning it to the composer's. If we say: "I am hearing music and being moved," we are not wholly attending for we cannot do two things at once: we cannot be taken out of ourself and contradictorily know we are taken out of ourself. In identifying with a piece it is ourself and not music which concerns us. In reality (or unreality) we are divided between one present and another; the divisions are so small they seem to melt together. Scientists say we are given an infinite variety of ideas per second. Were it possible to grasp only one of them and prolong the present indefinitely, we might blast through dried oils to bare canvas where centuries ago an artist posed the soul by which we know him now: himself, the man!

There are tourists incapable of looking at a masterpiece for its own sake. They bow into a camera, snap experiences never had, then rush home and develop these celluloid events so as to see where they've been. Sometimes the film turns out blank. What we wish to keep we lose. When not urged to possess we are free to love. Concertgoers who seek or manufacture memorable experience have missed the point. Admission of this fact eliminates the need for tears at a symphony. The concept of a non-existent past, or fears of a non-existent future rising from past learning, make us cry. Apprehension is a waste of time—it is only now and predicts nothing.

The same is true of the performer who comes between us and the work he plays. When moved by his own performance he is a "ham" without the objective control of projection. His immediate feelings becloud our appreciation. The composer has

not expressed his immediate feelings, for how could he weep
and simultaneously have the *sang froid* to notate his tears?
Such a production would contain about the same sentimental
authenticity as a high-school love lyric. Of the thousand reasons
for audience emotion, not one may have been apparent to the
composer.

A funeral march is not a funeral. Its author does not mean
us to weep (even *if* he did), nor to blur our reactions dream-
fashion. He clears the mist. If the gesture eludes us he is not
at fault. What seems complex may be an ultimate plainness to
which art transforms idea. But the nature-hating gimmicks of
our society have unaccustomed us to simplicity. The gesture
clarifies only what is contained within us: it is not in the music
that we perceive what we hear. Sympathy between the outer
sound and inner self ignites fireworks in some and lights no
spark in others.

Scales of appreciation have as little relation to intelligence
as facility for language has to musical gift. (There are brilliant
musicians who just can't begin to master foreign tongues, and
unmusical dullards who are proficient—though equally dull—
in several languages. The separation between what is called an
"ear" for language and an ear for music is really the difference
between two brands of extroversion; ears themselves are all
pretty much the same.) While enthusing over music, we sometimes see the so-called tone-deaf person looking as though he'd
missed the point of a joke. Jokes can be explained, perhaps, but
feeling art is the taste for a certain love. And love is the attempt
to unfathom a mystery. When this succeeds, love dissolves. A
superb paradox!

There is, probably, a comprehension that demands no set
answers. The mystery of a masterpiece is never fully fathomed.
In lacking the magic touch Clementi was monotonous where
Mozart excelled, though as craftsmen they were on a par. No
one will ever find sensible words for the difference between the
great and the merely admirable. Which is why masterpieces,

from one aspect, are all a bit boring: their multiple levels tax the effort of approach, and hard work is tedious. We often have greater affection for lesser products. We need not bother to decipher affection since total comprehension (assuming it's possible) sterilizes art. Besides, taste is unanalyzable. But if we dislike a work which we nevertheless feel to be great, we should know how to justify the opinion. This cultivation encourages the taste inherent in everyone. There is no good or bad taste, only taste. Unlike a bias, it seldom changes character, though sometimes it expands.

Can a listener let his mind wander, then come away the richer from subconscious exposure to music? Stimulus without concentration is useless for positive opinion, just as the beauty of dreams has small creative value next day. Like the church-goer who gets only what he brings and brings only what he comes for, the concert-attender must attend for the concert. But as for being enriched (attentive or not), he will find that music—as opposed to church—is oblivious to persuasion or morality.

Unconscious listening is more dependable. Carlyle maintained that if you "see deep enough . . . you see musically; the heart of nature being everywhere musical, if you can only reach it." In signifying only itself, music becomes a language translatable by the universal awareness latent in everything. This most complex of expressions is also the oldest and so appeals to our most primitive level, inexplicable through reason. At that level we all hear music the same way though surface reactions vary with social advancement. Tears and concerts, for instance, are recent Western distortions.

Frequently an unskilled listener or child penetrates more directly than a dilettante into new works. Nothing in the ear structure rejects unusual sonority. Children won't complain louder about the worthwhile than about juvenilia: they like or don't, without censorship or duty; only later do questions begin. We can grow nervous in wondering what art ought to be, and intellect alone will never inform us what it must be. No music is ahead of its time, but the public is often behind its time. The future doesn't tell. We must accept our music as it stands today, for the pronouncements of new decades upon our culture will rely on new tastes formed by the extra-musical phenomenon of social progress. The sole formula a musical layman need observe is: the conscious repetition of exposure produces true opinion. "Mature artistic judgment can result only from the love of art," to quote Roger Sessions. "Any judgment in the absence of love is sterile and therefore false."

For the music student or practicing performer this love is presupposed and he must go beyond it. Perceptive acuteness of the untrained is fine, but may be deceiving. A little knowledge is dangerous, and it is only fair to offer formal encouragement to aptitude.

Formal encouragement means a technical sharpening of the ability to enjoy music. There are all kinds of enjoyment (gay, macabre, passionate, sadistic, innocent, even boring), but none of them is passive. Active enjoyment is the comprehension that begins with memory. A popular song is retained through reaction when we whistle or dance but, for the student, music is a rigorous game with complex interplay. The rules are not beautiful in themselves but in their productive understanding. The beauty of production lies in form which, with music, is ordering specific processes of repetition and variation. Anecdotes about a piece are often given to laymen as aid to recognition, but only ear-training for landmarks within a piece provides the familiarity of scholarly appreciation. Ear-training is usually imparted mechanically with no ends for the means. Though no end in itself, without it even the talented grow insecure while following scores. And there are hundreds of more-than-adequate performers who don't know technically what they're doing. Knowledge of harmony designates tonal location within a piece, and this is the essence of form (at least in standard repertory). Counterpoint study helps distinguish more than one voice: every note of a master can be accounted for. Instrumentalists should attempt formal self-expression so as to follow other music without getting lost. The ear is probably best trained through copying entire scores by hand, or even in actual composition.

The usual music student won't, and shouldn't be, a composer. Inspection of the problems will, in Schoenberg's words, "give him only one pleasure: [that] of balance between the joy he expects from music and the joy he actually receives." The advice is good for listening with new ears to old music. By what standards does he judge the new?

A trained musician can listen objectively most of the time. But whatever his opinion of a new work's quality, he cannot say its performance was good or bad without the standard of previous performances by which to compare it. The test lies in whether the piece holds his attention. If it does, he wants to see the score. Then if he is still interested, the music works and is "good" for him. Nothing of much importance is accomplished overnight, and love at first sight is rare. Love at first hearing is less indicative than involuntary concentration. Both trained and untrained listener can learn to love just as jokes can be explained. When he hears right he will progressively amend his tolerance level, not with the intention of accepting all, but of acquiring discriminatory judgment. He can readjust to almost any diet. Of course, whatever opportunities are offered, their results are unsure: a horse led to water won't always drink. The best education has been used for negative goals.

There will always be varieties of listener good and bad, logical and sensual, even impermeable. These last need not be morally obligated. As for the others, if they enjoy themselves no harm is done. Reactions are never the same; no psychologist is permitted to say our musical comprehension is off balance, or to know if his vision of blue is the same as our blue. There is no invariable listening method, no universal language on our conscious plane. But some education is helpful in shattering false illusions. The shock is short-lived when illusions are replaced by ideas of how to judge for ourselves. It's even better to be wrong than unopinionated. Freedom of choice is achieved by the labor of understanding.

Music must be a necessity we seek, not a luxury taken for granted. Anything is allowed the fool who sees nothing and the genius who perceives all. For the connoisseur a certain knowledge of certain rules for a certain time will be of eminent aid in resolving enigmas.

An American, Charles Ives, composed a work called *The Unanswered Question*. Being a masterpiece, it is an answer in itself. Gertrude Stein did not hear it in death—but we can, while very much alive. If we don't like it, we can listen again. Then again. Resolutions will come through music of the present. That is the only way to know the past.

Buffalo, 1960

7
Composer and Performance

When the final note of a composition is inscribed the composer's struggle is over and so is his creative pleasure. This work was accomplished mostly in silence and alone. Yet music, to have meaning for others, must be played aloud, and the road from composition to audition can be rough and long.

After the thrilling rosy shocks a young composer experiences in rounding up musicians to decipher his early efforts, he recoils before a challenge: that of procuring adequate professional hearings. His elder colleagues are of little use here, being too busy with the same problem and inclined to envy their juniors. Which is why so many composers pursue with ulterior motives the society of performing artists rather than of each other.

An "established" author of music knows rather accurately how his work-in-progress will ultimately sound, so is apt to lose interest at its completion, or at least after its début; he is less intent on launching it than on starting something new. But the growth of a young artist depends on constant realization of his ideas; in order to learn, he must hear what he's written. This is easier said than done, especially when he writes for symphonic combinations. A piece commissioned for performance has smooth enough travel from manuscript to auditorium, though respectable execution is never guaranteed. When composed for its own sake, however, without anterior prospects of public presentation, the launching process of a new work—even by the famous—is complex, expensive, and interminable.

Excepting drama, music is the only art to require mediation between producer and consumer; and drama is less bound to interpretation since it is more visual than visceral and makes sense to one who reads it. But silent score-perusal provides only a general approximation: music needs to be heard to be "believed." Before this century, creative musicians themselves were middlemen when improvising in a patron's parlor. In our specialized age, a composer is usually just a composer and requires an interpreter. If he hustles he can generally find a soloist who will give him at least one public audition. But for the average young hopeful's unsolicited symphony, the following costly and time-consuming transactions occur between his last draft and first hearing.

Today a symphonic work of, say, twenty-five minutes takes anywhere from a month to three years to conceive, notate, revise, and orchestrate. That is the engrossing period of composition. Afterward comes endless hack-work. If the full score amounts to three hundred pages, a union copyist will charge up to a thousand dollars for its transcription into what is called "autograph." So the composer does it himself on translucent paper suitable for the cheapest method of reproduction. This paper, at twenty-five cents a page, costs fifty dollars.

Music calligraphy, a grueling technique in itself, must be scrupulously adept or the performer will not consider the manuscript. An hour per page (or three hundred hours for the whole) is average copy time. Photo-offset duplication comes to around thirty dollars a copy. If the young musician can afford it he has five copies made, and mails them, along with engaging letters, to five conductors—reputedly champions of new music. A year later his scores may all be rejected and returned, and he will try his luck with other conductors.

If perhaps his work is accepted by even a third-rate orchestra, he is of course anxious to hear it. As the extraction of the separate instrumental parts is his own responsibility, this will involve either two hundred more hours of painstaking copy, or around seven hundred dollars to a professional copyist, plus additional reproduction costs.

When the great day arrives, he spends another hundred on train fare and hotel bills in the town where the orchestra has welcomed him with scant publicity, attends an insufficient rehearsal at which he's consulted with minimal deference, and takes a bow after the concert that is reviewed with speculative competence. Then the sound dies out forever, his work sinks into oblivion: a Society-for-the-Propagation-of-Second-Performances does not yet exist! The unknown hopeful has spent maybe three years of lonely labor on a single piece, and maybe fifteen hundred dollars for an hour's practical experience; many composers of parallel development don't even achieve this much. For better or worse he has learned something in hearing his music live once, but the procedure is discouraging. For solace he always has the dubious but tangible write-up which, however accurate, is no more than desultory comment on his deepest thoughts.[1]

An uncommissioned work by the established composer is prey to a not dissimilar sequence, except that his publisher negotiates correspondence, exacts rental fees, and reports the performance to the performing-rights society, which pays a regular stipend. When the piece is printed he receives royalties from sale to invisible artists who may turn their questionable renditions into a recording to be broadcast later on the radio, from which it will be taped by music fans for their private use. By this time the composer's germinal impulse is so far behind him that he recognizes his music as a long-lost acquaintance with whom he

[1] Young composers understandably don't write large orchestral works much anymore. They compose for the excellent chamber groups in residence at colleges where America's most important musical activity takes place.

now has little in common. Sometimes he feels as though the vicissitudes occurring between creation and performance are hardly worth the trouble.

In any case, the definitive audition of all music transpires within the artist at work. No ensuing "live" representation coincides with this gestational notion—and it usually affords some shocks.

Composers are seldom surprised but often displeased with a performer's concept of their phraseology. They are often surprised but seldom displeased with a performer's concept of their tempo. Since music notation is inexact, all interpretation of it is different (occasionally better, usually worse) from what its originator had in mind. Nor is a composer's own public performance representative: he alters conceptions once his notes are brought from the introspective studio to expedient execution. These conceptions generally concern speed.

A metronome is an undependable criterion; the only designation which can't be misapplied is *presto possibile*. Tempos vary with generations like the rapidity of language. Music's velocity has less organic import than its phraseology and rhythmic qualities; what counts in performance is the artistry of phrase and beat within a tempo. A composer is never sure of tempo before rehearsal, for preoccupation with such a detail during composition slackens creative flow. Writing time corresponds in no way to performance time, and intuitions regarding the latter are, at best, approximate. Notation of a scherzo can need many days and pages, though it plays a few seconds.

Slow movements are successfully written in one sitting, but the impulse in fast music presupposes pitfalls because inspiration can't be sustained for long. A too-eager composer inclines toward technical padding in rapid movements, and is wise to heed Hemingway's warning to Marlene Dietrich: never confuse motion with action. The pulse of creation is rarely identical to that of performance. (Francis Poulenc once told me: "Robert

Shaw is not only my favorite choral conductor but my favorite musician of all time. His rendition of my music corresponds to the very action of the blood through my body!" Now this judgment from a composer is as rare as it is complimentary.)

Tempo indication is not creation, but an afterthought related to performance. Naturally an inherently fast piece must be played fast, a slow one slow—but to just what extent is a decision for players. If the composer happens to be the performer, so much the better. Rhythm and phrasing, nevertheless, do pertain to composition and are always misconceived (though sometimes beautifully), for as I say, notation is inexact.

When a composer determines his tempo as a final gesture to the product, he does so as an interpreter. Since tempo varies with the life of the times, his marking will ultimately suffer deviation. And since musical tabulation is inaccurate, his emotional conjectures will not have authentic translation into sound. The composer will never hear his music in reality as he heard it in spirit. Small wonder that his interest sometimes wanes when notation, or even formation, is accomplished. He prefers to compose something new rather than pursue the hardships of attaining—and disillusionments in achieving—good performance.

A moment back I mentioned that a composer's own performance of his music is not necessarily definitive. How often at parties he is confronted with requests like: "Do play us your new symphony!"—and when he explains that his symphony was not conceived for keyboard, and that anyway he doesn't recall how it goes, there's a disappointed reply: "You wrote it after all; you of all people should know it!" But on completing one piece he leaves it to begin another; it is his interpreter's job to master the technicalities and memorize the notes. Remember that composition and execution, though not mutually exclusive, do not go hand in hand. Some fine composers cannot play any instrument competently. And the true virtuoso-composer (Rachmaninoff, for instance) really has two professions: he must sit down objectively and *learn* his own music as he learns anyone else's: by practicing. As for obliging with a piano reduction of his symphony, or singing with skilled simultaneity the various male and female roles of his opera, his party-public must be equipped with a sophisticated ability for score-reading or they won't make head or tail of his behavior.

Musicians of the "popular" world maintain that composition and performance in a jazz solo constitute a single process; what is played is the same as how it's played. But this is not true formal creation any more than the improvised cadenzas in nineteenth-century concertos; it is only a technical trick demonstrating a facility for spontaneous variation on pre-composed tunes.

It may be that the expanding voyage from psychical germ to physical sound is necessarily a mutative process terminating, for a creator, in the shock of recognition. As with his audience, the initial visceral exposure to his composition is most decisive; and, like a jury, he cannot eradicate first impressions. The public, of course, does not experience this sonorous shock of recognition which is the relation between a seed's fertilization and its eventual blooming. Sudden wisdom gained at hearing thought in sound is not unlike the disturbing sensation most of us have experienced in unfamiliar situations: we feel sure this has happened before, but when?—in another life? Or like James Joyce who, confronted with the cold print in his first published book of love poems, exclaimed: "But these are not love poems at all!"

The public and composer hear in a less like fashion than members of the public among themselves.

The entire history of evolution is contained in the development of one human embryo. I like to liken the private and the public (the composer and his audience) to this process: a composer's work suggests the whole of creation as comprehended through Darwin, while the audience represents an embryonic version of evolution. No two listeners hear alike. Each takes away a shred of the composer's self. This shred is the listeners' own gestation, and though their pregnancy gives birth to children none of whom resemble each other, they all resemble mankind—that is, the evolutionary gamut. The most learnèd articles about music might not correspond at all to its composer's diagnosis; there is only one composer of the one work which has set off these multiple reactions, and by this time he is dead, or uninterested, or off somewhere writing something else.

He has gone away because the glamorous shock of recognition wears thin. He is soon accustomed to realities of "live" audition; these realities liquidate (or obscure) his first imaginary hearing by imposing one impression upon another. He can retrace the steps from conception, through birth, to performance (as Poe did in a post-mortem of his *Raven*, or Clouzot in his film on Picasso at work) only with an objectivity devoid of the "emotion" laymen are pleased to feature as artistic creation.

A second live performance, however, though possibly an improvement, seldom obliterates or holds surprises over the first. Since the composer is quickly used to the impurities of the initial aural surprise, a new and superior rendition can be disturbing when it does not match first impressions.

Most composers don't like concerts. Absorbed all day in their own music, by evening they aren't disposed toward anyone else's. Passive audience participation means sharing the breathing space, program-crackling, dubious thought waves, and distracted coughing of strangers, most of whom, when they pay attention, admire performance and not subject matter. Since the impresario of management has become the chief star of the music world and dictates program-planning to performers, who in turn must mostly ignore contemporary composers, there is small adventure in concert-going.

Management has arbitrarily determined the limits of taste;

the more popular executant artists conform by becoming sports-
men rather than musical servants. Repertory has dwindled to
about fifty proven masterworks of the past. So the public today,
being more concerned with the playing than what's played, is
less prepared to appreciate the three B's: Bach, Beethoven, and
Brahms, than the three C's: Casals, Callas, and Cliburn. As for
new composers, they are virtually left out in the cold, and have
little wish to patronize recitals of famous artists who unfailingly
execute (though each with a personal signature!) the identical,
standardized program of other famous artists.

Many a good composer, then, hears less "live" music than the
regular concertgoer, and some have a smaller repertorial knowledge of the classics than the average disk collector. The composer is, of course, for the most part, educated on classics like
everyone else, but after a certain point such works no longer
happen to be pertinent to his creative life. Being steeped in the
music of his own time, he is prone to take the past for granted,
with the result that years may go by without his sitting down to
re-hear, say, Beethoven's *Fifth*. This symphony, taken at long
intervals, is likely to exude more rejuvenated meaning for him
than for the lay public who hear little else and so have no
point of comparison. (My own artistic education was the
reverse of most in that the first valuable music I was exposed
to was of my own century. And I loved this music to a point
where the classics presented as formidable a blockade to me as
the moderns do to others; I took the sound of my day by
instinct, but needed education to the past: which demonstrates
—despite the impresario's protest—that a capacity for understanding is strictly a matter of familiarity).

Vast knowledge is a quality of the dilettante; it doesn't necessarily make a finer artist and in some cases can inhibit him.
When André Breton was asked why he never learned English
during his years in America, he replied: *"Pour ne pas ternir
mon français."* I have seen composers who, because they are
so intellectually conscious of how a piece should go, and so

avidly aware of the structural devices of others, become paralyzed when they undertake their own composition. Others are
inordinately prolific, having unshakable faith in themselves
rather than in the produce of others.

Unless he supports himself as critic or pedagogue, the only
concerts a composer frequents are those devoted to the chamber
music of himself and his colleagues, and even these prove
trying. They are privately subsidized programs presented to
small groups of modern-music *afficionados.* This elite public, in
the trend of the times, also judges all music more by its performance than by intrinsic quality. In the case of a new work,
only its composer is qualified to know whether performance is
good or not; even *his* judgment is disputable since, like his
audience, he has not the standards of previous performances by
which to compare the present one.

When his own music is not in question, he still attends these
small concerts less for enjoyment than to keep up, broaden his
outlook, estimate his rivals, maybe plagiarize an idea or two;
he is always in search of new material from either within or
without. Sometimes he comes to renounce his confrères as
sterile, and organizes a vogue for little-known but fertile
masterpieces of the past. The novelty of thrill is increasingly
rare as one catches up with existent literature, and it is seldom
that a familiar work revives the intensity of its initial impact.

A musical author is less occupied with production of pleasure
than with production, period! And he is less occupied with the
product's being understood than with its *not* being *mis*understood. His one aim is self-expression, and since this expression
is communicable only through mediation, he can just hope for
the best. But the best of performers (or mediators) remain
servile to Big Business, and their volunteering of new music
issues solely from good will toward the composer at the risk of
diminishing prestige with their public. So, as they seldom learn
such music, and then play it a single time, it has no occasion

to mellow in their brain, much less in the public's. How, then, can audiences *not* misunderstand a work heard but once and under debatable circumstances?

The elite public is on the composer's side, the general public is for the virtuoso; though both (whether they know it or not) estimate creation by performance.

A composer shuns the big concert from boredom, and is present at the small one from sheer loyalty. If his work is represented on either, he is reluctant to attend because, although mediocre performance is out of his hands, he is always held responsible and condemned. His interpreter signals him to rise, and he must smile hypocritically in acknowledgment of the feeble and misdirected applause.

When communication of his music has possibilities for being reasonably faithful to his intentions, he is still reluctant to attend—for other motives. There is a strange embarrassment in hearing one's music while others are present. A composer as audience to his own score usually doesn't listen to it so much as its interpretation: the recitalist's timing, phrasing, tonal beauty —or those many separate instruments uniting to raise life from a mass of black dots. In this he resembles the public which is alert only to performance, with the difference that the black dots are of *his* making—and he worries about them. In his nervousness over detail he hears only what goes wrong; what goes right is inaudible.

Audiences may get a better idea than the composer of his new piece in that they hear what "sounds" while he is aware of what doesn't "come off"; they absorb the whole while he hears separate parts and feels these parts are monstrously evident to everyone. If all goes well for the author, then he wonders if others are listening as he is. If they are not, he is nervous that they may have lost his message; if they are, he is nervous that they may have found his message. He perceives a spectral side of himself filling the hall with a sound he no longer controls.

This is intensely personal: he feels disrobed, defenseless, imagining others know his secrets; he is as uneasy at the possibility of the audience grasping the minutest discrepancy as at having his soul laid bare. There, of course, he is deluded: centuries will pass before psychologists decipher the symbolic tongue of music and expose, telepathically as it were, the creator's innermost thoughts. If music could be translated into human speech, it would no longer need to exist.

The ordeal over, the audience fixes the composer with bemused indulgence, somewhat astonished to find a man of flesh. Then they clap. Acclaim, though flattering and justified and even necessary, has no relation to the creative spirit. A writer is only a writer when he's writing. With the production behind him (the work of another man, so to speak) he feels public acknowledgment misplaced.

When his older works are played the composer hesitates attending because of a bittersweet nostalgia. There is little connection between initial impetus and final proofs: a publisher returns manuscript for correction, and the composer hardly recalls who wrote it! He may weep hearing his own songs, but it is less at the music's persuasion than from memory of himself as someone he once knew. That "someone" now is lost. The composer loses himself in each endeavor, and resultingly finds himself. Then he loses the music, for a printed song no longer belongs to its maker: he holds out his hand a while, but the sound escapes, disappears, henceforth to defend itself without a parent's guidance. When his song arrives in a concert hall the parent is uneasy that this half-recollected child will misbehave.

How then, and when, can a composer actually sit back and enjoy his finished works? Probably the nearest answer is: when he is alone with a phonograph, and a recorded rendition he approves of. Speaking for myself, years of phonographic in-

struction have made me come rather to despise recordings, and
to like collecting less than producing. Some musicians know all
about music except how to make it, so are obliged to collect for
pleasure. Most composers are too wrapped up in their craft to
live as the pedant who moves all around an art without attaining its enigmatic heart.

But the phonograph is a necessary evil, and gives a composer the opportunity to hear his music without stage fright,
or sitting in an audience and worrying over wrong notes. He
has, for better or worse, an unalterable performance. We have
observed that he quickly grows used to the first audition, and
that no eventual superior performance can obscure this—nor
even revive the period of formation.

Here is a personal example: In 1953 I wrote a twenty-minute
piece for the Louisville Orchestra, which commissioned and
recorded several such works yearly. As I was in France I was
secretly relieved at not having to attend any rehearsals, performances, or recording sessions, all of which can be painful.
I first heard the work privately on the final recording sent to
me, and was pleased to have notated my ideas succinctly
enough for authentic transference into sound four thousand
miles off. Qualifications I held about this performance were, as
I played the disk over and over, gradually eliminated, or rather,
absorbed into an overall effect as I now heard it undistractedly
in sound. Perhaps I subconsciously concluded that these dis-
crepancies were my intention. . . The only "live" rendition I've
attended of the work was under Eugene Ormandy with the
Philadelphia Orchestra, which is reputedly the world's most
sumptuous. By this time my Louisville listening habits were so
solidified that I could only consider the golden Philadelphia
tones as a kind of vague miscalculation.

So much for the sedentary sins of phonograph listening, and
for the virtuous complacency it provides to both layman
and composer. Live listening is naturally more exhilarating and
instructive than records, but can be so wounding to the com-

poser that he occasionally prefers to linger in the solitary realm of what Truman Capote names "sounds on the edge of silence."

But music, after all, is meant to be heard. (Stravinsky even maintains that all musical performance should be seen, and that closing the eyes during a concert makes one subject to irrelevant daydreams.) For the sake of a point, composers have here been shown more sensitive than they really are to the quandary of perfection. Like all artists, they are susceptible to appreciation and only hope for justifiable performance. Some feel greater joy in directing, conducting, and organizing tangible manifestation of their work than in actual composing.

When he can, a conscientious executant should always listen to the originator, no matter how inarticulate the latter. Though a composer may be an unskilled interpreter, his private keyboard performance gives an instinctive hearer the clearest skeletal sense of his works. My ideal impression of all music is in my own mediocre playing and singing: imagination rectifies my technical inexactitudes. Another performance is more exciting, but completely divorced from me.

Composers are frequently interrogated about how it feels to hear their own music. Is it thrilling? For myself, though only a mildly curious auditor of a piece I've heard many times, I'm always uneasy. It is less disconcerting to accompany my songs on stage than to sit with an audience. As collaborative performer I am directly responsible for what is heard, so must concentrate on the business at hand. Hence I am not prey to the creator's distraction, nor do I even feel to be a composer while performing my own music. Whether my performance is capable is irrelevant to my nervous system.

Nerves apart, the composer doubtless has a larger, more extended post-creative thrill than any other artist in that his product alone involves double emergence: a "double birth," if I may say so, or a "double life"; the subjective birth through mind to paper, and the objective life through sound. Even a play has life on paper—but never music. Though one can scarcely say that music on paper does not exist; it simply has two existences while other arts have one.

To sum up: A composer's function has been purely achieved at the completion of a given work. From then on impurities arise. The music will not fully exist until sounded before some audience. When the composer is not his own interpreter he is usually entrepreneur for his auditions, a job both arduous and disheartening. When he performs himself, his conception is only one of many, and not necessarily the most authentic because (though he may be a fine conductor or instrumentalist) he cannot simultaneously be an author and an interpreter: one stops where the other begins. Nor is he used to listening to himself from outside; he hears primarily in silence. He is no more responsible for his own rendition than he is for that of others.

As occasions increase for listening dispassionately to his own music, he is less startled by disparities between what he hears and what he calculated. His calculations, however, are notated in an imperfect system, so while his music is played he always has surprises. They are pleasurable or not, depending on the variance of performing artists. Pleasant surprises are tastefully novel alterations of speed; unpleasant ones are betrayals of rhythm and phrase.

A performing composer can be his own worst enemy. Since a written sequence of notes is only theoretically explicit, its interpreter necessarily takes liberties. An available composer can be consulted at rehearsal, though he is never quite sure how his music should go; his job is to create, not to explain.

Composer and public are comparable to the evolutionary premise: ontogeny repeats philogeny. All listeners contribute, in a sense, their individual definition of a given musical work.

Composers often avoid concerts because they are saturated

with their own music, because they are weary of standardized programs exalting virtuoso rather than creator, and because (when their works are represented) they are intimidated. The intimidation is either from dismay at a possible bad performance for which they are blameless, or from schizophrenia at hearing notes which no longer directly concern them and over which they've relinquished control.

They are usually a little impatient while their music is played: it sounds better or worse but never the same as what they heard in the inner ear. When impatience becomes gratifying, it's a transference of how they hope their audience is reacting. Their own reaction is doubtless most objective when alone with recordings.

Although acclaim is agreeable, it is foreign to the composer's basic elation. For that elation is exercised only in the hermetic act of writing music, and is of such unique magnitude and mystery that it is not only irrelevant but impossible to depict in words.

Philadelphia, 1959

8

Four Questions Answered

"It is a good lesson—though it may often be a hard one—for a man who has dreamed of literary fame, and of making for himself a rank among the world's dignitaries by such means, to step outside of the narrow circle in which his claims are recognized, and to find how utterly devoid of significance, beyond that circle, is all he achieves, all he aims at."—*Hawthorne*

A composer is always in the act of composing. Before the first draft reaches paper, a subconscious preparation occurs. The man can be pregnant, so to speak, with simultaneous but unrelated ideas; some of these eventually crystallize, to emerge in notation. Both the gestational and conscious formations are part of the composing act. Although the long secret "pregnancy" may end in feverish and rapid parturition, there still remain the mundane tasks of orchestration and interminable copy. While engaged in such tasks, ideas for new works are overlapping within the composer's mind.

His conscious procedures are a tedious responsibility. Of necessity, he spends much of his life alone, attending to a thousand post-compositional details mostly involving India ink and transparent paper. These details fall midway between his creative and professional lives.

Professionally he frequents publishers, performers and their managers, sometimes critics—and, if he writes for theater—directors, producers, sometimes actors. His social hours are often passed in the same company, or with fellow-composers and artists in other fields. He is not mysterious to such acquaintances.

But to the public—if it stops to consider him—he and his friends are, at best, eccentric. An artist who momentarily quits his specialized orbit is taken aback at how little the outside world is concerned with him. Even to the musical public a composer does not exist—he has been dead for a hundred years. This public is unaware of the creator's violent interest in a vocation excluded from the so-called "normal." The artist and the everyday world feel they speak different tongues. When that world does admit an artist's existence as human, it seems more curious about how he creates than what he creates.

Therefore, the questions so often asked of a composer by outsiders are not those which primarily occupy him (except the ones about money). The four most usual are, in order of frequency: Do you write popular or classical? Do you compose at the piano? How do you make a living? Where do you get your inspiration?

The first question is settled by defining the terms. The second is one of fact, and might be answered "yes" or "no." The third also is a factual matter, but needs elaboration. The last is the most problematical, and no reply is really satisfactory. My answers may include a good deal more than the interrogator bargained for. But perhaps, just once, a composer should respond in good faith.

Do You Write Popular or Classical?

Reply to this depends on a patient estimate of the questioner's intelligence and education level. A composer knows the intent behind the question, and that answering "classical" will satisfy.

Nevertheless, he is irritated by ill-defined terms: the words "popular" and "classical" signify nothing in themselves.

What the totally uninformed outsider means by classical is music played to a race apart, behind the closed doors of a concert hall. And popular is everything heard on a jukebox.

What the somewhat more-informed person understands by classical is really semi-classical, which he interprets as a mixture of popular and classical. Semi-classical, in turn, concerns anything from *Rustle of Spring*, or Stephen Foster, or just a half-remembered pianola tune from days of yore, to the *Warsaw Concerto* or lush arrangements of Kern and Gershwin.

When the sophisticated layman says "classical" he implies music notated by masters, rarely contemporary, occasionally symphonic, usually operatic. "Popular" to him means music of the people (whatever that means! In this case it's generally Folk Song which, of course, does not involve a composer).

All of these conceptions are vague, not to say incorrect. The musician is exasperated by such undefined terms. Especially when he himself has no alternative definitions.

Music written today is never classical. The word applies to a particular era in history. Some true classical music, like Beethoven's *Fifth*, is popular to a non-musical public. Other true classical music, like Mozart's C-major Sonata, is popularized through arrangements. Certain romantic work thought of as classical, like Tchaikovsky's Piano Concerto, is also popularized. A variety of modern classical music, like Stravinsky's *Firebird*, has true popularity in concerts. Other modern classical music, like Khatchaturian's *Saber Dance*, is heard unaltered in popular locales. Much "popular" music never achieves popularity, while a popular song like *Stardust* is almost a classic.

The composer would like to reply: "My music is not classical. I hope it will be popular. But it will never be popular in the sense you mean. So let's say it's classical!" This would elicit only a vacant stare from his interlocutor. And rightly so. As terms, "popular" and "classical" are senseless because they are interchangeable.

The substitution of "serious" for "classical" is not much of an improvement. Some composers of popular music take themselves very seriously, while some "serious" composers are not at all serious and seek only popularity. Much popular music, in both senses, is serious indeed!

Nor is the substitution of "jazz" for "popular" a correct translation. Jazz, like classical, describes the special style of a special period.

Even within their respective orbits, these two seemingly opposed music worlds have trouble defining themselves. One of these worlds in the present day contains two extremes: Rock 'n' roll for the proletariat, Progressive or Cool for the intellectual. (Cool and hot are really the same; the difference in terms lies in the psychology of he who employs them.) Since 1900 this music has variously been called Jive, Ragtime, Barrell-House, Blues, Torch, Sweet, Swing, and Bop. Many of these names derived from verses that dictated a style of vocal delivery which ultimately influenced instrumental performance. None of them can yet be comprehended by an all-inclusive word.

Today's "serious" music world has at times been self-defined as *contemporary, modern,* and *new* (all of which are equally fitting to the "popular" world). The difficulty with the phrase "contemporary music" is that nobody is quite sure with what it is contemporary. "Modern" is more unsure—it indicates the whole epoch from the Industrial Revolution to now, and has come generally to mean dissonant, though dissonance itself is hardly modern. As for "new," it suggests anything recent. But new music is not timely if made in the style of Mozart.

Nor are "commercial" and "non-commercial" cogent. Nowadays many "popular" musicians starve, while some "classical" ones make a fine living on TV.

As "popular" is a generic, and "classical" a specific term, they are mutually exclusive. How can they be accurately replaced?

Two alternatives come to mind, both stemming from the attitude of the questioner himself. "Classical" music is invariable in that the same notes are played for different performances; "popular" music is variable in that notes are improvised according to the player's mood. As for the listener, he can regard either music with equal seriousness or equal disdain: both make a bid for posterity; both are part of music anyway. So why not simply call them "variable" and "invariable"?

"But," says the "popular" musician, "classical music is 'long-hair'"! This he does not mean, however, as an objection. Indeed, he has probably been more influenced by advances made in recent long-hair music than the latter has been influenced by him. In point of fact the two musics employ interchangeable devices: "long-hair" uses jazz instrumentation and sometimes improvisation; progressive jazz itself uses strict notation. Yet both musics remain psychologically separate in the public ear. Why not, then, concede the issue—for it is only a matter of hairs split from the same head—and call them "short-hair" and "long-hair"?[1]

Neither of these definitions is more confusing than the accepted terminology. The new slogans unite the two fields, but that's all right if the general music lover learns to take his variable music a little more seriously, and his long-hair a little less so. In the end, of course, we'll all revert to former ways, with the reassuring assumption that most people know perfectly well what we're talking about.

Do You Compose at the Piano?

Some composers always use the piano, some use it part-time, and some never. Prescribed working systems cannot insure good results. Methods are less important than their outcome.

To the layman today, nevertheless, music is *the* intangible

---

[1] Now in 1966 the definition only holds if you switch hairdos. The Mod coiffure is longer than Liszt's, while the serious composer cuts his hair as befits the professor he's become.

art because it is heard and not seen. He is more intrigued by a musician's workshop than by that of other artists. He accepts without question the painter's brush, but has a notion there is something lacking in a composer who writes at the piano, even if the composition is *for* piano.

This notion results from a romantic misconception of past composers who are pictured as strolling with the muse down a country lane and notating their inspiration on the spot as a full-blown composition. Of course, music used to be comparatively simple, and harmonic relations could be heard by the inner ear without need to confirm them at a keyboard. But inventors of today's complex sonorities don't usually rely on imagination alone. Stravinsky even maintains it is unmusical to write away from the piano, for music deals with sound and composers should always work with sonorous references.

His opinion probably applies just to the creative act of composition, not to the technical craft of orchestration wherein a sort of "practicality" is the keynote. Orchestration at the piano would be implausible since it requires choices of color combinations extraneous to that instrument; unlike composition, it is an acquired talent.

A composer on the opposite stand declares that the discipline of avoiding a piano sharpens the inner ear and eliminates the ornamental solutions which obscure true invention.

Now musical composition, though it always deals with sound, does not *primarily* deal with sound, but with organization of ideas eventually expressed through the direct language of sound. Ideas can occur today in country lanes or in bathrooms, as they did to composers yesterday. The difference is that as they seldom occur fully realized, their ultimate usefulness might not be ascertained until they are remolded at the piano. Which doesn't mean a composer rambles over the keyboard hoping his fingers will shape his theme; nor will good ideas necessarily come through improvisation. It means that once an idea is found, association with the sound element may indicate the natural "tone" of the idea, and then aid in subjecting this "tone" to the metamorphosis of formal development.

Music designed to be played on a piano is certainly more effective when calculated for what the piano can do. It's safe to assume that all masters of virtuoso keyboard-writing (from Scarlatti, through Chopin, to Rachmaninoff) realized their material in keyboard contact. Can you imagine the glittering roulades of Liszt as being thought up in silence? Nowadays we emphasize the instrument's more percussive qualities, but this is no less "pianistic."

It does not follow that to write effectively one must know how to play the instrument for which one is composing. And if composing for a group of instruments, there is even less reason, since it goes without saying that no one can play them all at the same time. A musical author is trained in orchestral theory: the physics of sound as pertaining to relationships of color, balance, and weight of various solo or masses of instruments. He is also trained to write characteristically for individual instruments according to their possible range, their happiest tessitura within this range, their shading potential and dynamic restriction. Nobody has time to master each instrument with consummate skill, and still compose. Half-mastery inhibits and limits. The theoretic possibilities are studied, then applied.

Nor does it follow that a composer who is an accomplished performer writes best for his instrument. On the contrary, his facility in performing (and hence in writing gratefully for the instrument) can induce laziness about purely musical problems, and allow technique to camouflage a flimsy structure.

Conversely, a composer who does not play a given instrument might happen upon aspects of its use that would not have occurred to the virtuoso. Hindemith, for example, a violist who never composes at the piano, writes keyboard works which do not sound difficult, but don't always "feel right" under the hands. An interpreter must divine this new concept of his instrument. A literary instance is in *Lolita*: because Nabokov's native tongue is Russian he lends our language a dimension unimaginable to authors reared in English.

Most complex pieces by composers who write at their desks—particularly those of the twelve-tone school—are basically contrapuntal. Polyphonic problems are inclined to be theoretical, and thus more easily solved in quiet.

The only other kind of music written away from the piano these days is (like much of Thomson's) so harmonically plain that it needs no reaffirmation outside the composer's head during the thinking-out procedure.

So, if a musician is going to compose on an instrument, the most logical is one that can sound two or more notes simultaneously (unless he is writing for single voice). As a result, most composers have at least a passing acquaintance with piano performance. Once an idea comes to them, as often as not it is worked out formally at a keyboard, even when the idea is not to be employed in a keyboard piece. Orchestration, however, since it concerns imagined sound and color-mixtures foreign to the piano, is a silent operation.

How Do You Make a Living?

It is sad to report that on the list of ways in which composers do or don't earn a living, purely musical composition is at the bottom! If they pick up a little money as composers, it will be less from areas where music is performed for its own sake, than from collaborative fields where music functions as decoration. The lower its importance in these fields, the higher its monetary value; and the more anonymous a composer, the greater his fee. Television pays extremely well; Hollywood pays very well; documentary films pay fairly well; backgrounds for legitimate plays, less well; ballet, still less; and modern dance, hardly at all, even when the work is included in repertory. (In each of these realms the union executant can earn many times more than the composer whose music he is playing.) Those who live on income from concert hearings alone are exceptions to be counted on one hand. (The show-tune author is another category with other considerations.)

A composer's living obviously derives from either musical or non-musical jobs. Thomson goes so far as to elaborate on the supposition that "every composer's music reflects in its subject-matter and in its style the source of the money the composer is living on while writing that music . . . [although] the *quality* of any piece of music is not a function of its author's income-source."

Both musical and non-musical jobs impel a composer to compose in his spare time. Non-musical jobs can be literally anything: David Diamond once had to live as a soda-jerker although his music was played by leading orchestras. The other extreme, John Alden Carpenter, headed a Chicago coal company.

Extra-compositional musical jobs are critical journalism, public performance and organization of performances, teaching and lecturing, publishing and editing.

Certain composers live on unearned income from their families, private donors, prizes, commissions, subventions, and foundation fellowships. Some have managed to exist from such sources for much of their lives, though music written in this subsidized freedom was seldom heard. Artists are all rare birds, and the composer who eats from the just rewards of his labor—notably royalties and performing-rights fees—is the rarest of all!

One can't generalize about how birds *should* eat, any more than about their procreative habits or the meaning of their song. What is beneficial to the penguin is catastrophic to the parrot. If a composer teaches, who can say how his song would sound if he didn't? When psychoanalysis is completed nobody knows how a patient might have ended without treatment—

perhaps much the same, but older, and with the wisdom (or lack of it) gained only with passing years. Occupational disease will nonetheless pollute the music of an author who specializes too long in an extra-compositional domain, no matter how close this domain seems to his creation, or how lucrative. Like doctors of disease, American composers are inclined to specialize even in their field of pure composition. General practice is more prevalent in professional Europe than here, where it implies a double life.

Once when Aaron Copland was in Hollywood to write a film score, he appeared at a concert as composer-pianist to play his knotty and difficult *Variations*. Afterward, who should turn up backstage but Groucho Marx. "What are *you* doing here?!" asked Copland. "I didn't know you liked this sort of music. I write two kinds. Don't tell Mr. Goldwyn, but I have a split personality." And Groucho replied: "Oh, he doesn't mind, so long as you split it with him."

The relation between the life and work of an artist is always fascinating. From a certain standpoint the two existences have no connection. The artist today is more or less in a dilemma from attempting to coördinate his inner and outer lives—and this reconciliation will not, of course, occur while the twentieth century is as it is. Yet creation continues withal. Whether the artist's social temperament is contained in this creation is not the subject. The public, however, is permitted to see *its* temperament reflected through the creation of others, though it doesn't always pay for the privilege. Perhaps this generality is beside the point.

Two generalities can be made without question. Most composers have extracurricular talents which they like practicing for money and a change of air whenever possible. Also, they have better business heads than people think.

Ideally, all creators should be granted opportunities for adjustment, with finances sufficient to permit them freedom to do the work for which they're equipped when they feel like doing it. No one outside the movies has ever proved that an artist works best on an empty stomach.[2]

The equivalent of "egg-head" does not exist in foreign tongues. Europeans are proud of their cultural heritage; the humblest knows the names, if not the work, of his country's chief intellectuals. I came back to Paris the day of Gide's death: the whole city was in mourning. The Finns idolized Sibelius beyond the proportions of our film star glamour build-up.

Americans, on the other hand, feel a certain embarrassment about art. We have always been a practical country and our earthy traditions linger. Unless a commodity gives tangible returns we are doubtful of its worth. We cannot weigh music for its monetary values nor judge it for concrete meaning, so we ignore our musicians and offer no government help.

Tentatively in the thirties there appeared an official recognition through the Works Progress Administration. At that period American music came into its own. There was no provision for creative music as such, but composers, collaborating with sub-sidized performing groups (especially the Theater Project), developed a functional simplification of style which characterized it as "American," and thus shook off two hundred years of foreign influence. This germinal thrust produced budding men who are masters today. But when the WPA's nourishing light was extinguished, they were left again to shift for themselves.

Maybe it is a credit to our culture that we have some of the greatest orchestras in the world, even if they are isolated examples. Less than one fair-sized city in twenty has a sym-

2 What this essay owes to Thomson's *The State of Music* (1939) is embarrassingly evident. The scene has nonetheless shifted for us all. Most composers, if they want, can now land well-paid jobs in universities. By their second year they've begun to believe what they teach, and by their tenth they're rich and (except for Milton Babbitt) obscure. I'm for the University Composer only if he's not expected to know how to teach. He should be given money and time in exchange for only his presence.

phony, and only six or seven contain a half-permanent opera company. The artistic vitality of our few larger centers is nothing compared to the hermetic cultural ignorance in the rest of this huge rich land.

All of our arts need support drastically. Much of our brightest young talent is obliged to forsake any idea of a career in order to subsist. Private foundations alone (and they are increasing) will never be able to underwrite all the needs of the intellectual American surge. Every large nation except ours has government-sponsored symphony, theater, and opera, in which young interpreters and creators are encouraged to experiment and grow and flower.

To complain that genius is stifled by federal participation is to contradict historic fact. Artists have always been inspired by commissions. Mozart once wrote his father: "I haven't yet sunk so low that I'll write a piece that hasn't been paid for in advance!" An artist does his best if unhampered by material problems. He is happiest at liberty to work when and as he wishes. This is not the case in America today.

Of course, the government shouldn't tell him what to do; official doctrine, by definition, lacks humanity in questions of art.

The French, with their glib Gallic wit, have said: "America is the only country in history to have gone from barbarism to decadence without an intervening civilization!" This *bon mot,* however untrue, should shame us into the actions which we, as a country, are more than capable of accomplishing.

Where Do You Get Inspiration?

No doubt what the questioner really means is: Define greatness. To him, inspiration is a miraculous element given by the muse to that chosen few who receive it and produce great works. The muse is thought to relieve this production of all effort.

The questioner forgets that he too is open to inspiration in his work. Yet, as he sees it, the artist's inspiration is special because it makes "lasting beauty." The lasting ingredient sets it apart for the layman, and makes it great. He doesn't always consider that great and living works have been born of no conscious inspiration, while deeply inspired ones have turned out to be utterly banal. Greatness is not the effect of which inspiration is the cause. We are all inspired, but we are not all great.

Balzac said: "The artist is like everybody else, but nobody else is like him!"

An artist doesn't necessarily have deeper feelings than other people, but he can express these feelings. He is like everyone else—only more so! He speaks with a Formal Sigh.

Quite literally, inspiration is nothing more than the act of breathing in. When we breathe out, we expire. An expiring artist is extraordinary if he has a good day, but this is not dependent on his inspiration.

"What is a poet?" asks Kierkegaard. "A poet is an unhappy being whose heart is torn by secret sufferings, but whose lips are so strangely formed that when the sighs and the cries escape them, they sound like beautiful music."

Inspiration could be called inhaling the memory of an act never experienced. The ensuing exhalation of the true artist is a marvelous copy of distorted recollection; imitation of what never existed; stealing of old masterpieces recalled through blurred glasses; misquotations of angels wrongly overheard; expressive notation of something expected which never arrives; the prevention of a crime. It is also none of these.

Is inspiration inventive? Perhaps, in some cases, but rarely for geniuses of interest to laymen. The power of invention seems rather to be granted to minor workers who conceive basic ideas later developed by great men. Rimbaud even dared say that genius was a faculty for clever theft. Genius is seldom original.

Why is one composer great, and another of equal competence, less great? Is the latter less inspired? Not necessarily. All this is talk around the subject—not about it. Nobody from Socrates to Freud has offered a completely logical explanation for the productive nature of great work. Such explanations are inevitably bathed in personal adjectives, evasive and variable as individuals.

Inspiration, as such, is no special concern of the composer. There is nothing much he can do about it anyway. He takes it for granted and goes on from there. However, he can do something about the tailoring of his technical resources. If his craft is not ready to construct a suitable lodging for the eventual visit of Inspiration, Inspiration will turn around and leave.

Brahms one day was confronted by a lady who unctiously inquired: "How do you make your slow movements so beautiful?" He replied with his legendary gruffness: "Because the publishers order them that way!" He was unconcerned with the hoped-for response which would have been: "Inspiration falls from heaven in my dreams."

Alas! Music of dreams becomes trash in the morning. Anyone can discover beautiful noise in revery. The composer's job is to communicate an organization of this sound. Inspiration through dreams is less dependable for the artist than for the prophet. How many times will a composer awaken full of wisdom, to find that as the day progresses his ecstasy evaporates when given utterance, and at nightfall only banalities have been scribbled? The work of art seldom springs from a gratuitous source.

Inspiration doesn't come *to* the artist, but is already *in* him, and comes *out* of him. His task is to provoke—and then employ it coldly. He can only assume it, and allow his brain to control it. Sometimes a whole piece is born seemingly through an impulse of the heart, perfectly formed without effort or change.

Other times pure logic shapes the inspiration to make the piece work. To "work" it must convince the intelligent listener of where he is at a given moment so as to comprehend the consequences at another moment. This requires the formal device of fusion with technique—what the French call *métier*. Since music is always Now, and since the listener should always be unconfusedly aware of his location within this Now, he should be *un*aware of the fusion. Unawareness comes through integration rather than camouflage. The composer should not be concerned with explaining this; however ingenius his elucidations, they are sometimes suspect and always irrelevant. A piece must defend itself without its mother's guiding hand. That such a piece turns out to be successful proves nothing of its artistic worth, and inspiration *per se* is independent of its value. Inspiration can be quite corny.

Since it comes from within, the spirit's light is blinded by the light of the world. Four bare walls provide the artist's best studio. A forced use of exterior stimuli produces embarrassing bromides—as when painters attempt (often so unsuccessfully) to depict sunsets. Gertrude said: "I like a view, but I like to sit with my back to it."

As with monks, composers work from habit sprung of driving urge. And as with monks, the revelation which produced the urge is not oft-repeated—only assumed. Divine fires do not blaze each day, but an artist functions in their afterglow hoping for their recurrence. Meanwhile he applies his tools to resculpt the initial urge into a variety of shapes with the clearest economy. And the monk repeats his prayer whose sense expands as he matures; he cannot always speak with God, but he can ponder on Him. The explicit economy of sound is for composers what silence is for monks. "Genius," as Shaw put it, "is one-tenth inspiration and nine-tenths perspiration." Monks have plebeian chores, communal misunderstandings; little of their life is ecstatic contemplation. Nor does an artist mildly await a tangible manifestation of the Creator Spirit, but works daily with and for its invisible presence.

Inspiration, moreover, may be a dangerous distraction. One cannot do two things at once—look at a sunset and compose a sunset. A flash of lightning in the night can illuminate, for one second, a whole landscape down to a blade of grass. The propelling flash! An artist spends his time in reconstructing the landscape from memory, from within—a landscape wider than nature. His inspiration is involuntary.

He need not strive to be sincere and personal; we assume that these one-faceted virtues are already his. He should be honest and objective. Whether the proceeds of his honest objectives appear inspired, and ultimately prove great, is beyond all control.

Philadelphia, Summer 1959

VARIATIONS WITHOUT A THEME

to Joseph Adamiak

"Lest we neglect to add a little more confusion . . ."
—*Paul Goodman*

9

Francis Poulenc

A Souvenir

Like his name he was both dapper and ungainly. His clothes
came from Lanvin but were unpressed. His hands were
scrubbed, but the fingernails were bitten to bone. His physiognomy showed a cross between weasel and trumpet, and featured
a large nose through which he wittily spoke. His sun-swept
apartment on the Luxembourg Gardens was grandly toned in
orange plush, but the floors squeaked annoyingly. His social
predilections were for duchesses and policemen, though he was
born and lived as a wealthy bourgeois. His villa at Noizay was
austere and immaculate, but surrounded by densely careless
arbors. There he wrote the greatest vocal music of our century,
all of it technically impeccable, and truly vulgar. He was deeply
devout and uncontrollably sensual.

In short, his aspect and personality, taste and music, each
contained contrasts which were not alternating but simultaneous. In a single spoken paragraph he would express terror
about a work in progress, hence his need for a pilgrimage to
the Black Virgin's Shrine at Rocamadour; his next breath ex-
tolled the joys of cruising the Deauville boardwalk. This was no
non sequitur but the statement of a whole man always inter-
locking soul and flesh, sacred and profane; the double awareness of artists, and of their emulators, the saints.

And, like artists, he was also a child; his self-absorption was stupefying. I recall once in Cannes his monologue to a baffled bartender about a series of triumphant modulations he had penned that afternoon. I remember also a river of tears as he listened to a record of his own *Stabat Mater*. "Robert Shaw," he wept, "is the greatest performer of our time: his tempi correspond to the very motion of my blood." And I remember a pair of elderly female instructors from the Tours *lycée*, each sporting a shirt and tie, who came for tea to his country home. While his big, liver-spotted hands popped tiny raspberry tarts into his mouth—washed down with *tilleul* (he seldom touched liquor)—he held forth on private Paris gossip, then talked for an hour about orchestration, all this to uncomprehending listeners, including the chauffeur, who was also at the party.

Yet he was not intellectual. Indeed, as a composer, he was never concerned with poetry's meaning beyond its musical possibilities. Which is why his songs surpass those of, say, Auric, who *knows* too much to release instinct. Songs are nonetheless a collaboration of both poet and musician. And though Poulenc is sung the world over, his chief bard, Paul Eluard, once told me that those songs obliterated the tunes he himself had heard while writing the verses. Which did not keep him from printing:

> *Francis, je ne m'écoutais pas*
> *Francis, je te dois de m'entendre.*

Because Francis was a friend, indiscriminately, generously! (He taught me more than anyone long before I dreamed of knowing him.) Both man and music were delicious—an adjective now suspect to the brainwashed public alerted to disrespect what it might understand or like. The very nature of Poulenc's art is to be liked and understood, which is therefore its momentary defeat.

So, although joyful by inclination, he nursed that special melancholy of the successful ones who are no longer admired by the young. Yet he did not attempt (as others may, if their powers wane) to seduce youth by adopting its mannerisms; his language remained constant. Self-centered though he was, he still remained one of the few composers I know who wasn't bored by the music of others. He regularly studied old scores while keeping his heart open to new trends.

Now that heart has killed him. Curiously, it was not his heart but his liver that plagued him during his later life (as it plagues all Frenchmen), in this case largely psychosomatic. When he was half finished with his "Carmélite" opera, there was a question of being denied the rights by Bernanos' estate. His organs grew paralyzed, he retired to a Swiss hospital where his circulation all but stopped and stigmata appeared on his wrists. He wrote farewell letters to everyone, exclaiming: "In the Middle Ages I'd have been burned alive for less than this!" When the rights were finally granted, he recovered overnight and completed the work, which has since glorified our international stages. There again was the contradictory child.

That child said: "We put words to music; but we must also put to music what is found in the white margin." In translating that marginal whiteness Poulenc, like Ravel, became not different but better than anyone else. Nobody in Paris can do it now. Not since Ravel's death in 1937 (I was ten) can I recall being so disturbed as by the news of Poulenc last week. For Poulenc had inherited Ravel's mantle, and today in leaving us he has taken with him the best of what remained in musical France.

February 1963

10

Arthur Honegger

*A Reappraisal**

He had the kindest face I've ever known, and an unaffected
intelligence which served as both balm and kindling to his
dozen pupils—of whom I was one during his final years. Those
years were nevertheless charged with both physical and moral
torment which he dissimulated (at least with us) except for
an occasional clenched fist or tired sigh. The quality of lucid
restraint glimmered also through the surface fury of his art, and
made him (thanks also to the somewhat sentimental and
"visual" texts he often chose) the most accessible of so-called
modern musicians for the general public.

For this reason, eleven summers ago, the French crowned
Arthur Honegger (although he was Swiss) their National Composer, voting his music as that most likely to survive the mil-
lennium. The following autumn a curtain was pulled, not only
on his life but on his work; nobody—not even the average
Parisian to whom he was perhaps the one *known* composer—
has talked much about him since. Those mid-fifties were already
dominated by the traditional revolutions of the young even as

* This was a review for *The New York Times* of *I Am a Composer*, by
Arthur Honegger. (Translated from the French by Wilson O. Clough in
collaboration with Allan Arthur Willman.) New York: St. Martin's Press,
1966.

124

Honegger and his friends had dictated the mid-twenties' tone, not so much in denigrating as in ignoring their elders. Nowadays the life span of new generations has shrunk to about five years, and musicians grow ever more quickly in and out of vogue. Unlike painters, death does not increase their market value. Except for Bartók (who was hardly cool in a debtor's grave before he was taken up internationally), no composer since the war has died with impunity—meaning with glory. Some, of course, like Griffes or Satie, are "discovered" by the intelligentsia a few decades late; others, like Ives or (to an extent) Poulenc, come in for revivals by the amateur. Neither category of listener seems yet inclined to disinter Honegger, although it had been his life's desire—and here maybe was his tragic flaw—to attract both the great mass and the elite through the same pieces.

Of those pieces, the one which most realized his desire, *Joan of Arc at the Stake*, seems now as frozen as a Griffith spectacular, featuring what Virgil Thomson once called "that least musical of instruments, the spoken voice." Yet Thomson cited *Pacific 231* as among the five most significant works of our first half-century. That piece has not, however, remained noticeably in the concert repertory, while performances of a gem like *Pastorale d'Eté* are rare as hens' teeth. Certainly Honegger's String Symphony does not go unheard, and his oratorio, *King David*, is practically a staple in our more elegant Episcopal churches. Though all in all his music no longer fills a need for most audiences, particularly the young, and the young constitute the one public a *maître* most longs for.

This ostracism personally touched the gentle musician during his last years when (despite being such a vastly "appreciated" creator) he decided to publish some rather melancholy verbal reactions. These he modeled on Gide's *Corydon*, using as his duologistic foil Monsieur Bernard Gavoty who, under the pseudonym of Clarendon, is still France's most redoubtable old-guard defender. Their conversations now reach us in translation some fifteen years later with a resonance not unlike the music's: personal and poignant, bold and witty, a trifle old-fashioned.

The personal poignance lies in the composer's pessimism. "A few years hence the musical art as we conceive it will no longer exist," states Honegger, who goes on to deplore the performer's precedence over the composer: music now "comes nearer the domain of sport than of art." Not twice but twenty times he reiterates "that we are living in the last stages of our civilization; inevitably, these last moments are painful. They will be more and more so." He would advise young hopefuls against the profession of composer: "It is a mania—a harmless madness," a lifetime of dedication which will reap scant glory and even less money. The talks read like the laments of an unknown failure; indeed, the first five chapters are variations on the title "Complaints." Not until the book's halfway point does a certain humor appear, albeit ironic.

His bold wit stems from this irony. Arthur Honegger was the most withdrawn—the least *mondain*—of that group named *Les Six* who, as we know, were promoted by Cocteau in the twenties as *Enfants Terribles* of a compound mentality, but who in reality soon went their six separate serious ways. Honegger's way was not like Poulenc's toward the salon and Roman ritual via Diaghilev and Latin liturgy, but toward mass culture and the Protestant ritual via professional pedagogy and vernacular Old Testament sagas. He did once collaborate (and gorgeously) with the stylish Cocteau, though his constant unqualified admiration was for the prose-verse of the much stuffier Claudel. His recollections of these and other working unions are warmly recounted in later chapters, as are snappy judgments of Lady Music Lovers and the dubious necessity of snobbery.

If the book seems a touch old-fashioned it is not so much in his wise bromides about matters professional. Composers when they're not composing have always voiced pretty much the same complaints in different words; rather it is in his assessment of the future, *i.e.*, our present. Sixteen years ago he declared: "I strongly fear that the twelve-tone fad—we already see its decline—may initiate a reaction towards a too simplistic, too rudimentary music. The cure for having swallowed sulphuric acid will be to drink syrup." Certainly he had a blind spot—or was it a pang of jealousy?—about the newest Terrible Children. Still, greater than he have uttered worse, and anything, even a shopping list, is important if scribbled by a genius. Whether Honegger was or not remains to be seen.

11

Random Notes from a Diary
(1961–1966)

to Frank O'Hara (1926–1966)

"I will always love you though I never loved you. . ."
—*Frank O'Hara*

I.

The hardest of all the arts to speak of is music, because music has no meaning to speak of.

For whom do you write your music?. . . Art for art's sake is hardly fashionable, though is there a better sake? But even should such a motivation exist (it probably doesn't), it would apply more to meaning than to purpose. Actually, composers compose for someone, but they're not always sure for whom. Alexie Haieff says we write for the friends we love. Or is it an imaginary listener we search for?—a person from the past, or ourselves in the future? In any case, not for ourselves in the present. Just as diaries are always made to be seen by other eyes, so all composers write for an audience, if not necessarily what the audience wants to hear—or thinks it wants to hear. They also write for commissioners; assured performances plus palpable pay counteract their dreamy apathy. (Good dreamers make bad artists.) In fact, all of my musician friends agree that money is their chief stimulation.

Does writing music help to get things out of your system?. . . Self-expression, as people call it, is not a purge. Artists obviously express what's in them, but the fact of clarifying it on paper doesn't mean it's no longer in them. Besides, any living thing can "express" itself; an athlete in action doesn't *think* of his muscles; a robin fashions, without knowing, the tone and life in her sky-blue egg. Murder may be provisional medicine to a maniac, but a few months (or days) later he'll not seek new releases, he'll commit another murder. A woman having borne a healthy child won't necessarily say she'll never have another (mothers don't join book clubs until their children leave for college). Similarly, an artist, having said something, has really only found a *form* in which to say it. Many great ones spend their lives repeating themselves in different colors.

I'm not convinced that artists ever advance, much less grow. What they know they know from the start; each work is a new way of saying the same thing. Their obsessions don't change, only their modes of emmission. Nor do they always know what they've said. Corot once answered a lady who was searching for hidden meanings in his work: *"Non, Madame, la peinture est plus bête que cela."*

Good music?. . . It depends on where you stand (one man's meat, etc.). The point used to arise through confusing art with entertainment. They've now been fused by intellectual and commoner alike. The only bad rock 'n' roll is that which doesn't distract delinquents from switch blades. Nobody cares about posterity anymore.

Nevertheless art (as it used to be called) is an aristocratic affair. One cannot demonstrate that the average man experiences—or can be trained to experience—those reactions which

make up a work of art, or an appreciation of that work. For the
first time ever he can have it all free, and rejects it. The world
feels an innate suspicion and jealousy for the artist, for the
artist has ripped open a protective curtain to display what outsiders most resent: himself.

Are you your work?. . . Am I my work? No, I was it. Not even
while in the act? While in the act some poison part drains off
forever while I now remain paradoxically weaker and stronger.
So, yes, while working, I'm it, or at least it's *in* me, but while
inside it's unhealthy. Once notated, interest lags (and this very
phrase could never attract me again—I'm cold to compliments
on bygone tunes). But spirit lags too. Empty now, but not
enough: dregs stay. My life was and will be spent in scraping
clean such stinking residue to create a vacuum. Yet to create
a vacuum is, in a sense, to fill it. An artist is slave to irony.

An artist is no more self-involved than other people; he just
shows it more.

Am I of the earth? I am not you, nor them, nor even my
work, for it becomes it. What can I leave? I am only my
name. . . Art, said Braque, is made to disturb, while science
reassures. I might be content that years from now my song
could act as a balm, though that song today leaves me, its
maker, dry.

Do you do your own orchestration?. . . Why is this an
enigma? Because study of musical notation is not a Liberal
Art. All collegians should learn instrumentation, though, conversely, composers don't need the Liberal Arts. (Yes, I do my
own orchestration.)

Where is music going?. . . Nowhere at present. Eventually,
though, it will follow, as it has in the past, wherever a great
monster leads it. His way will not be one of invention but of
synthesis, a gathering of trends into a communicable whole.

He will write not from vogue but from necessity, and he will *get the necessity over*. His voice will sing out, avoiding theories. For art's not abstraction of ideas but incarnation of ideas. We talk all around it, but only the thing itself explains the thing itself. What music "should" do is nothing next to what it does.

That monster is not yet around. Meanwhile, music's definition—for the first time ever—requires expanding. Among the young it has come to fill logical, not emotional, needs. I cannot object: one may resent evolutions but not deny them. My own language, however, remains one of "expression," a damning word today.

There's no real audience (emotionally pleased) for contemporary music now. Concerts serve a new purpose for their little public: what's played is not important, what *happens* is. Boredom too has become an art. The reaction music is supposed to produce is the reaction it does produce, so any reaction is the right reaction.

How can we be sure of how well you really knew all those dead French people?. . . "To know well" means an exchange between two participants of permanent portions of themselves. In the four or five meals I had with Cocteau, or fewer with Eluard, in certain street encounters with green-eyed strangers who took me by the hand to painful hotels, in chance tearful meetings with Tchelichev or an hilarious single supper with John Latouche, I felt a contact, a generosity, a participation, a heat, a curiosity, an indelibility which permit me to say I knew and know and will always know them well. Meanwhile I'm indifferent to some people I've seen daily for twenty years; they offer neither growth nor anecdote. *To know* has to do with intensity, not habit.

How much time did it take you to compose that?. . . I don't know, ten minutes, eighteen years. Would you despise me if I said it was easy? I can only tell exactly how long it took to put on paper, though what difference does it make? But then, what difference does anything make?

II.

"Those dying generations—at their song. . ."
—*Yeats*
"Poetry is not concerned with thoughts, but with words."
—*Mallarmé*
"Man was given the Word to hide his thought."
—*Malgrida*

Musical tempo depends on the tempo of living, as the tempo of living indicates that of language. No one is sure of speech's speed in Chaucer's day; philologists surmise it to have been radically slower than ours. In a hundred years we will speak more rapidly. We perform music of the last century faster (and stricter) than it was probably played then. Similarly, a performer's instinctive choice of style is dictated more by the sonorous shape of his spoken native tongue than by a conscious attempt to penetrate the composer's mind.

Nor are performers necessarily qualified interpreters of their national music. Subjectivity is detrimental to execution. The German Gieseking played Debussy more "comprehensibly" than any Frenchman I ever heard.

The speech of a nation originates from its music, not the other way around.

Consider how the generous Italian ripple is so like the Italians, and the gutteral Arabic sensuality like Arabs themselves; how the suave, smooth, logical, arhythmic French tongue is like the French, German like Germans, or the somber Flamenco spurt resembles Spanish. And how Americans have altered English to fit their irritable jazzy innocence.

The musical public of a nation resembles its performers, as the performers resemble the composer. An Italian barber knows his country's music better than our typical opera queen. Everyone sings in Italy: audiences identify to such an extent with the stage expression that they must be suppressed from audible demonstration, whereupon they rise to dance on their seats. Dance in Spain is the germ of Flamenco song; the grave, harsh howl results from a bodily spasm. The Spanish sing with their feet as Italians dance with their throats. Cocteau: "The Flamenco singer spits out flowers of fire, then extinguishes them beneath his heel."

The French are more visual than aural, and have an unequaled sense of painting, flower arrangement, and food preparation. They *see* their music. They too are verbal during a concert, but in discreet Gallic commentary *on* the music rather than loud Latin association *with* the music. Germans, contrariwise, have little innate visual sense (their architecture, their grocery displays, are unappetizing) but, in their weird way, have the highest auditory appreciation in the West. At concerts they are mute as marble; nothing stands between them and the composer (if he's German) except the performer whom they psychoanalyze on the spot for a deeper understanding of the sound's secret sense.

Americans, like their music, combine Italian extroversion, Spanish kinetics, French discretion, and Teuton neurasthenia.

The art of translation lies less in knowing the other language than in knowing your own.

When Fauré was asked the ideal tempo for a song, he answered: "If the singer is bad—very fast." Composers haven't necessarily preconceived ideas of interpretation. (A composer has the first word, never the last.) When a singer is good and has worked, that singer's concept is usually "right" on some terms, so the composer has little to suggest; if the singer is bad, nothing the composer might say will help much. A song, more than any musical form, is subject to varieties of legitimate interpretation by virtue of the performer's sex and vocal timbre. I'll accept—and be pleased by—radical variants from a singer which I'll refuse from a violinist or conductor.

I feel guilty about what I do best—setting words to music. Because it comes easily (meaning naturally), I feel I'm cheating. Still, it isn't *my* hand that has wings but another Ned Rorem's; I sit back impotent watching his hand err and triumph.

The hand works to fill a void. Whether the work is good doesn't matter.

I know music—I don't know *about* music. Yes, I write songs. This does not mean I *know how* to write songs. I can show you how to make a perfect one, but not a good one. (Oh, I *do* "know how" to compose, but that's all. If I've anything to "impart," I'm unaware of it.)

Yet I was once arbitrarily named the best song-writer in the world. For me to agree would be to take the way of movie stars who believe their own publicity; that ends in suicide. Not to agree would be the way of humility; humility isn't for artists; it leads to complacent mediocrity, another route to suicide. The right road, then? No one is ever "the best," they are all absolutes. One is only better. But by whose definition?

Composers may be profligate but never stars. Singers may be stars but never profligate.

Speech is man's most confused and egocentric expression; his most orderly and magnanimous utterance is song. This quasi-paradox is demonstrable by cocktail party (or even organized simultaneous) talk versus vocal "pitched" fugatos. Consider how our ear at a noisy gathering can select, can distinguish and *focus* more nimbly than our eye; how we hardly wait for *him* to finish so *we* can start; how non-pitched voices become a babble of words which at best are weak symbols for ideas; how "ideas" in music are more than words can say; how boring singers speaking are; and how cohesion lacks in any coinciding speech, even when purposefully planned as in my play "The Young Among Themselves." Then consider how any group singing, by virtue of precalculated tones, immediately makes sense; how a singer loses his identity inside a greater identity; how the thread of a frugal notion weaves itself into a vaster fugal frame which in turn turns and shifts so that idea as Idea grows negligible within the Fact.

Speech, the human voice, is a gramophone record. Some records are longer than others, but our mechanisms ultimately set back the needle. Sooner or later you've heard all your best friends have to say. Then comes the tolerance of real love.

Love is a mystery which, when solved, evaporates. The same holds for music.

Once I said that the Sonata was a legitimate form, but that Song was a bastard progeny of two mediums. Amendment: Song is a mule, the sterile product of the union of two species. No song can reduplicate itself, each has its own rules.

Poulenc's carp, like those spawned under Louis XVI and still swimming at Versailles (minus their rifled gold collars), is a jewel with a single perfect facet illuminated by that slow-flipping tail in the left hand.

The French popular song has triple meter with narrational subject matter in A-B-C form. ("When our love was young he looked at only me; then he slept with the concièrge's daughter; now, though I've killed him and await the guillotine, I'm content knowing we'll soon be together in heaven.") The American popular song has duple meter with static subject matter in A-B-A form. ("He doesn't love me, maybe he will tomorrow, but he doesn't today.") The American relates a state of mind, the French a state of body. The difference between America and

France is, in the largest sense, the difference between Protestant specialists and Catholic non-specialists.

My predispositions are French. People sometimes show surprise that I, being a songster, feel no affinity for Schubert. His *lieder* leave me absolutely cold.

I was more moved by the death of Billie Holiday than by the death of Landowska. For if Landowska was closer to the world in which I move, she was farther from the time in which I live, while Billie was part of my day. During twenty years I *felt* her more than any classical performer. Bill Flanagan says (and I say it too about him) that I plagiarized Billie's spontaneous inflections and froze them into compositional idiosyncrasies.

All music is a sung expression, and all instruments attempt to emulate the human voice. The piano in trying hardest failed most nobly. Yet instrumental composers have gradually ousted lyrical ones, so the latter impose their talents elsewhere— notably on high drama.

Now it doesn't follow that he who has fashioned singable songs will also construct workable operas. Opera's main challenge is theatrical, not vocal. Yes, no one writes songs anymore and everyone writes operas, but few of those operas come off, despite all sorts of wild electronic invention. Possibly it's because the proscenium arch (except for framing dancers) is finished. A brand new outlet for the medium itself is more indicated than the constant refurbishment of musical devices. That outlet will be through a projector. Because the future of opera lies in the movies. What the static aria once achieved on stage the mobile close-up will accomplish on film, with an additional introspection that our age demands. We will no longer avoid poets as librettists: their every explicit, even fussy, word will be understood.

Europe's idols are historical tragedians, ours are recent

comedians. Yet even Italians today have forsaken "legitimate" theater and take Marilyn Monroe as seriously as they once took Eleanora Duse. Imagine a new Marilyn, dubbed, singing the words of, say, Frank O'Hara, as set to music by. . . !

Could unheard melodies be truly sweeter? Intelligence is silence, truth being invisible. But what a racket I make in declaring this.

III.

"Consistency is the hobgoblin of little minds."
—*Emerson*
"I brought my harp to the party
But nobody asked me to play."
—*From a Gracie Fields song*

Artists don't seek reasons. They are all by definition children, and vice versa. Like children, alas, they are always showing you rough drafts.

Criminals are saints *manqués*. Saints are artists *manqués*. Artists are criminals *manqués*.

Does sound come to our ears, or do our ears go out to sound? Earshot is a meaningless word; our ears go out to the horrible beauties all about. Or *should* go out. Really we hear just our heartbeat, taste just the tongue, contemplate our navel, smell nothing but our upper lip, and feel not even our own fingertips. Perhaps they're all we have.

Twenty years ago after the première of a Ben Weber work at an I.S.C.M. concert I asked Lou Harrison: "Was that piece of Ben's twelve-tone?" "Sure. Couldn't you tell by the way he avoided saying so?" Imagine such an attitude today!

Of course I was part of that serial movement—the part that talked against it.

They're all writing the same piece. At the moment that piece is for intoned speech with small chamber group, and resembles —according to the instrumentation—Pierrot Lunaire for parties (Boulez's ice-cubey xylophones), Pierrot Lunaire for barnyards (Berio's cackling woodwork), or Pierrot Lunaire for Sunday School (Babbitt's organy loud-speakers). Pieces that evoke—as these do—extra-musical rather than intra-musical stimuli are always preferable to vice versa, *i.e.*, those point-blank imitations of the above three B's that grow indistinguishable from each other.

The difference between Reactionary and Conservative is that the former uses traditional devices unchanged, the latter uses them freshly. Bill Flanagan points out that within the catalogues of, say, just Barber and Moore, both tendencies exist. To name only vocal works: *Knoxville* and *Baby Doe* are conservative, *Vanessa* and *Wings of the Dove* are reactionary.

I could hope for my music to be thought dateless, like much of Satie (his *Gymnopédies* sound as new today as in 1888); not astonishing for when it was composed, like much of Ives; or pleasantly nineteenth century, like much of Menotti; or quickly *démodé*, like much of the current Academy. But without Time, unmannered. . . They tell me I'm gazing into a mirror of the past. But mirrors are faithless: if they reflect the truth vertically they inevitably lie to breadth, since right and left are reversed, and become wrong and left. Am I right to be left and wrong?

(Salt Lake City) Late last night, alone—or so I thought—in a studio of Music Hall, I was reading through the Purcell

Fantazias at the piano. Gradually the music grew out of focus. I grew scared, stopped playing, yet sound continued. Wasn't I alone? Stepping into the hallway I heard more clearly what seemed a distant wheezing tuba. I peeked into the concert hall and witnessed this: eight ladies, each armed with a double-bass, were performing unison exercises under the tutelage of a ninth. My ear had heard brass. Unexpected sonorities aren't always identifiable: middle-C on the piano, caught and sustained electronically after the *ictus*, is acoustically identical to the French horn. Pop a green grape into the mouth of an unalerted blind man: he'll think it's a soft marble or a butter ball.

Joseph Adamiak is apathetic (in the style of the times— though what times weren't? we know only our century) because he can't break the block between ambition and work questions. Work questions, because he needs to be right, before the fact rather than after. Like Auric he's hamstrung by logic. A real artist (if you like generalities, and who doesn't?—though how an artist should work provides the sole axiom in the universe without laws) is unafraid of vomit, of decontrolled shrieks, doesn't fear being bad. He *doesn't not*: he *does*—and judges only results, never possibilities. Blind before risks, he can run only correct ones despite himself—that's his definition; chance and choice to him reverse their accepted meanings. But Joseph, not wanting to be wrong, ends by not wanting.

Taste, like intelligence, can stifle the abandon needed for "getting on with it," although intelligence and taste are not akin.

Yeats: "Man can embody truth but he cannot know it."

The chore of beauty. Maybe what's worth writing can't be written. Why try? As a frame of reference. Art isn't *that* important! Life—to quote Arnold Weinstein—isn't everything.

Fame brings more pleasure than the so-called creative act it irrelevantly celebrates. Fame while it lasts is complete, while creation (how I despise that ill-used word!) is often unfaithful, always imperfect.

Perfection is no more a requisite to art than to heroes. Frigidaires are perfect. Beauty limps.

My frigidaire has had to be replaced.

Stravinsky, being a great man, is always right. The Great don't make mistakes—or what makes them great? Like Marlon Brando's changing physiognomy, all that Stravinsky does is right, even when we know he's wrong.

The Great don't innovate, they fertilize seeds planted by lackeys, then leave to others the inhaling of the flowers whose roots they've manured. A deceptive memory may be the key to their originality.

Adjectives for music (velvet touch, golden tone, delicious) are tactile, visual, or oral—but not aural, how can they be?

Poets are worse off than composers because they earn even less, and because their craft does not demand the hack-work that eases tensions. A poet's main problem is what to do with those other twenty-four hours a day.

My music is a diary no less compromising than my prose, though nobody seems to hear it that way. A diary nevertheless differs from a musical composition in that it depicts the moment, the writer's present mood which, were it inscribed an hour later, could emerge quite otherwise. I don't believe that composers notate their moods, they don't tell the music where to go—it leads them.

Why do I write music? Because I want to hear it—it's simple as that. Others may have more "talent," more "sense of duty" (Lukas Foss now admits this). But I compose just from necessity, and no one else is making what I need.

Yet we're all afraid of being misrepresented, as though we didn't misrepresent ourselves every minute.

To start writing about your life is, from one standpoint, to stop living it. You must avoid adventures today so as to make time for registering those of yesterday. Of course, musical composition is also the sacrifice of social living; but though it too is possibly autobiographical, it is not necessarily retrospective— at least no one can prove it to be.

Echoi is a depressing masterpiece. It contains much that since childhood I've precisely thought of doing but never sat down and did. What more can I say? Today I feel a certain pride that Lukas' *Time Cycle* was conceived in my apartment which he sublet during my Buffalo year.

It's New York and late summer. The strongest remaining pleasure is, toward seven in the evening on our way to supper at the Waverly Inn, to pass beside those mauve and moulting Rose of Sharon trees that hang over Bank Street.

Réverdy maintains there is no love, only proofs of love. By the same token there is no poetry, only proofs of poetry. There is no universe, only proofs of the universe, and those proofs are art. . . People are suspicious of an artist who will not verbalize his work: they feel he is evading the issue. Yet a phrase like "let the music speak for itself" is corny only because it's true. My performers, in singing for their supper, may starve. Still I'm beginning to miss the solitude of work, the silence of my own sounds.

Appendix

These are the musical programs following my lectures which took place in Baird Hall and the Capen Auditorium of Buffalo University.

1. December 3, 1959
   Lecture: "Composer and Performance"
   REGINA SARFATY, mezzo-soprano, and NED ROREM, piano, in a recital of American songs by Aaron Copland, Virgil Thomson, William Flanagan, Theodore Chanler, Igor Stravinsky, and Ned Rorem.

2. January 26, 1960
   Lecture: "Four Questions Answered"
   ROBERT BRINK, violin, and DANIEL PINKHAM, harpsichord, in a program of American works composed for the artists by Ervin Henning, Henry Cowell, Alan Hovhaness, Klaus George Roy, John Bavicchi, and Daniel Pinkham.

3. February 25, 1960
   Lecture: "Writing Songs"
   DOROTHY ROSENBERGER, soprano, PATRICIA ORESKOVIC, mezzo-soprano, STANLEY CURTIS, tenor, ALLEN GILES and NED ROREM, pianos.
   > *Socrate* by Erik Satie (in English translation by Virgil Thomson and Ned Rorem)
   > *Sonata for Two Pianos* by Igor Stravinsky
   > *Sicilienne for Two Pianos* by Ned Rorem
   > *Canticle No. 2 (Abraham and Isaac)* by Benjamin Britten

143

4. April 7, 1960
   Lecture: "Pictures and Pieces"
   WILLIAM MASSELOS performing twentieth-century music
   for the piano by Carlos Chávez, Anton Webern, Aaron Cop-
   land, Ben Weber, Alan Hovhaness, Erik Satie, Ned Rorem,
   Charles Ives.

5. May 17, 1960
   Lecture: "Listening and Hearing"
   Members of the faculty of the Music Department in two
   performances (the first, a world première) of Ned Rorem's
   "Eleven Studies for Eleven Players," commissioned by the
   Slee Foundation and dedicated to the memory of Cameron
   Baird.

6. November 10, 1960
   Lecture: "Is New Music New?"
   DOROTHY ROSENBERGER, soprano, VAHAN KHANZADIAN,
   tenor, RICHARD SEIGEL, baritone, GORDON SALISBURY, boy
   soprano, ALLEN GILES and NED ROREM, pianos, and a
   chorus of students directed by GERARD REINAGEL.
   Four Dialogues for Two Voices and Two Pianos (text,
   Frank O'Hara) by Ned Rorem
   He Who Says Yes (Der Jasager) by Kurt Weill and Bertolt
   Brecht (English translation by Ned Rorem)

7. December 15, 1960
   Lecture: "Song and Singer"
   PHYLLIS CURTIN, soprano, and NED ROREM, piano, in a
   recital of songs by Francis Poulenc (*"Telle jour, telle nuit"*)
   and Ned Rorem.

8. January 26, 1961
   Symposium: "More Questions Answered"
   ARTHUR GOLD and ROBERT FIZDALE, duo-pianists, assisted
   by GEORGE D'ANNA and JOHN ROWLAND, percussionists.
   Sonata for Two Pianos by Francis Poulenc
   Cing Epigraphes Antiques by Claude Debussy
   Sonata for Two Pianos and Percussion by Béla Bartók